FOLLOWING GOD FULLY

FOLLOWING GOD FULLY
An Introduction to the Puritans

Joel R. Beeke
and Michael Reeves

REFORMATION HERITAGE BOOKS
Grand Rapids, Michigan

Reformation Heritage Books
3070 29th St. SE
Grand Rapids, MI 49512
616-977-0889
orders@heritagebooks.org
www.heritagebooks.org

Scripture taken from the King James Version. In the public domain.

Printed in the United States of America
22 23 24 25 26 27/10 9 8 7 6 5 4 3 2 1

Library of Congress Cataloging-in-Publication Data

Names: Beeke, Joel R., 1952- author. | Reeves, Michael (Michael D.) author.
Title: Following God fully : an introduction to the Puritans / Joel R. Beeke and
    Michael Reeves.
Description: Grand Rapids, Michigan : Reformation Heritage Books, [2022] |
    Includes bibliographical references.
Identifiers: LCCN 2021040889 (print) | LCCN 2021040890 (ebook) |
    ISBN 9781601786524 (hardcover) | ISBN 9781601786548 (epub)
Subjects: LCSH: Puritans.
Classification: LCC BX9323 .B4379 2022 (print) | LCC BX9323 (ebook) |
    DDC 285/.9—dc23
LC record available at https://lccn.loc.gov/2021040889
LC ebook record available at https://lccn.loc.gov/2021040890

For additional Reformed literature, request a free book list from Reformation Heritage Books at the above regular or email address.

The Puritans, as a body, have done more to elevate the national character than any class of Englishmen that ever lived. Ardent lovers of civil liberty, and ready to die in its defense—mighty at the council board, and no less mighty in the battlefield—feared abroad throughout Europe, and invincible at home while united—great with their pens, and no less great with their swords—fearing God very much, and fearing men very little—they were a generation of men who have never received from their country the honor that they deserve.

—J. C. Ryle

(introduction to Thomas Manton's *Works*, 2:xi)

Table of Contents

Preface

Twice God said of Caleb that he followed Him fully—once before the forty-year wilderness journey, and once after (Num. 14:24; Josh. 14:14). As a fruit of Christ's righteousness imputed to him, Caleb was enabled by God's grace to follow God fully all the days of his life. To follow God fully means to follow Him in these ways:

- *Constantly.* That's what Caleb did. Caleb didn't just follow God when it was easy. He refused to yield to murmuring rebels who surrounded him for forty years in the wilderness. He was determined to follow God constantly, perseveringly, patiently, unswervingly, in season and out of season (2 Tim. 4:2), even it if meant rejection by his peers.

- *Sacrificially.* To follow God sincerely means following Him with all your heart regardless of the cost because He is holy, beautiful, lovable, and worthy to be worshiped. It means being willing to sacrifice all for Him. That's what Caleb did; he loved not his life unto death. When the Israelites picked up stones to put Caleb to death because he said that Israel should go into the land of Canaan, Caleb didn't flinch, compromise, or negotiate. He would rather die than disobey God.

- *Consistently.* Caleb didn't pick and choose which commands of God he felt like obeying, but he did whatever the Lord told him to do. His obedience was not a partial, halting obedience, but a consistent, complete obedience. Every area of his life was fully devoted to God—including all its particulars. Like the Puritans, Caleb believed that God's law must be reduced to its particulars, since to offend in one point is to offend in all (James 2:10). Caleb did the particular duties he was commanded to do at the time, rather than rest in a general assent to the whole of the law while excusing any momentary lapse or disobedience.

- *Exclusively.* After forty years of wandering in the wilderness and after fierce battles with the Canaanites, Caleb was rewarded in Joshua 14:14 "because…he wholly followed the LORD God of Israel." After all those trials, difficulties, and temptations, Caleb is described as one who wholly followed the Lord, who allowed no other gods in his life. He didn't waste his life, but lived exclusively for his God, the only God. By grace, he lived life to the fullest—for his God, by his God, unto his God's glory.

Despite their shortcomings, the Puritans strove to be Calebs (and Joshuas) before God, to follow Him fully in every area of their lives. Like Caleb, they were but men, beset with the common infirmities of our race; but they were men of faith, and that set them apart from many others. It was saving, justifying faith that set Caleb, Joshua, and the Puritans apart from their contemporaries—that is, faith lived out, salvation worked out with fear and trembling. By grace, they followed the Lord constantly, sacrificially, consistently, and exclusively. Hence the title of this book.

What follows is an introduction to the Puritan story—to their lives, their faith in God the Father, their focus on Jesus Christ, and their sanctification by the Spirit. It unveils them as the bride of Christ and shows how they lived their daily lives. It teaches us what we can learn from them—both from their Caleb-like convictions and from their weaknesses.

Welcome to our introduction to the Puritans in forty-four short chapters. May God use this book in some small way to make us a bit more like Caleb and the Puritans so that we would follow them insofar as they followed Christ (1 Cor. 11:1).

PART ONE

Who Were the Puritans

1

The Myth and Foundation
of Puritanism

"The frozen chosen." "Haunted by the fear that someone, somewhere, may be happy." "Baptized in vinegar and weaned on a pickle." That's the latter-day view of the Puritans. The very words Puritan and puritanical are slung about as bits of verbal mud.

In fact, the word was coined in the sixteenth century as a term of abuse. For the average Englishman, there was the Roman Catholic "Papist" on one side, and the "Precisionist" or "Puritan," on the other side. The term suggested a nit-picking, holier-than-thou party of men who considered themselves purer than the rest. It was certainly not a fair description: those it was applied to clearly never thought of themselves as pure, but far from it, as their constant testimony to their own sinfulness and imperfection demonstrates.

Who, then, were the Puritans? Perhaps John Milton put it best, when he spoke of "the reforming of the Reformation," for that was the united goal of all Puritans: a continuation of the work of reforming the visible church, the lives of church members, and the society in which they lived. It was not that they thought of themselves as pure or fully Reformed; it was that they wanted to reform in an ongoing manner what in the church and in themselves remained to be purified. They wanted reformation, while they frankly disavowed the idea that the Reformation could ever be thought to be finished and complete.

Right but Repulsive?

Before we tell their story, some of the mud that has been thrown at them needs to be wiped off if we are ever to understand them.

For one thing, they did not even look like what we think of today as the stereotypical Puritan. We might imagine the Puritans always wore black—and scowled. That is how their portraits show them, for that was their Sunday best—and sitting for portraits was a formal thing, often far from pleasant. But on other days they might wear any one or more of the colors of the rainbow. In the fashion of the times, John Owen, perhaps the greatest Puritan theologian, would walk through Oxford with his hair powdered, wearing a velvet jacket, with Spanish leather boots.

Nor were they a crowd of inveterate sourpusses. Edmund Morgan writes: "Contrary to popular impression, the Puritan was no ascetic. If he continually warned against the vanity of the creatures as misused by fallen man, he never praised hair shirts or dry crusts. He liked good food, good drink and homely comforts."[1] As the description of Owen shows, they also liked to dress well according to their means and station in life.

A Scriptural People

The most important trait of the Puritans that contributes to their being misunderstood today is the one that really did unite them all: their passionate love for the Bible as the written Word of God, for Bible study, and for listening to sermons that faithfully and fully expounded the Bible. This was the foundation of their faith, their thought, their teaching, their worship, and their daily lives.

Again and again we hear of Puritans happily traveling hours to hear a good, substantial sermon, and of how they thought a good Bible study better than an evening's reveling. Sermons were usually an hour or longer, but even two-hour sermons were not unheard of. Laurence Chaderton (1536–1640), the extraordinarily long-lived Master of that nursery of Puritanism, Emmanuel College, Cambridge, once apologized to his congregation for preaching to them for two hours straight. Their response was to cry, "For God's sake, sir, go on, go on!" To people who have never experienced the reading and hearing of the Word as something thrilling, such behavior sounds at best boring, and at worst deranged. But the people of Europe had been without a Bible that they could read in their native tongue for approximately a thousand years. To be able to read God's own words, and to see in them such good news that God saves sinners, not on the basis of their holy intentions or good works, but entirely by His own grace, was like glorious sunshine bursting into the dark, gray world of religious guilt and human misery.

To fail to understand the Puritans' love for the Bible—that they loved to read, hear, study, memorize, sing, discuss, live by it, and to relish the Spirit's power that accompanied it—makes it impossible to understand the Puritans themselves. Puritan Richard Greenham suggested eight ways to read Scripture: with diligence, wisdom, preparation, meditation, conference, faith, practice,

---

1. Edmund Morgan, *The Puritan Family: Religion and Domestic Relations in Seventeenth-Century New England* (New York: Harper & Row, 1966), 16.

and prayer.[2] The Puritans gathered up what they found in the Book of God and applied it to all areas of life. They viewed this sacred Book of all books as the God of the universe speaking to them personally as their Father, comforting them as their Savior, and directing them as their Sanctifier, giving them the truth they could trust for all eternity. They regarded its sixty-six books as the library of the Holy Spirit bequeathed to them and empowered by Him to renew their minds and transform their lives in and through Jesus Christ, to the glory of God.

The Puritans called believers to be Word-centered in faith and practice. Richard Baxter's *Christian Directory* shows how the Puritans regarded the Bible as a trustworthy guide for all of life. Every case of conscience was subjected to Scripture's directives. Henry Smith said, "We should set the Word of God always before us like a rule, and believe nothing but that which it teacheth, love nothing but that which it prescribeth, hate nothing but that which it forbiddeth, do nothing but that which it commandeth."[3]

If you read the Puritans regularly, their Bible-centeredness becomes contagious. Though their commentaries on Scripture are not the last word in scholarly exegesis, the Puritans show us, better than many later works, how to vow wholehearted allegiance to the truth of Holy Scripture. Like them, you will become a believer in the living Book, concurring with John Flavel, who said, "The Scriptures teach us the best way of living, the noblest way of suffering, and the most comfortable way of dying."[4]

To them, the Bible was more precious than life itself. Take, for example, an account of a well-known Puritan event: "Roaring" John Rogers preaching a sermon in the pretty little village of Dedham in the east of England. Here John Howe records Thomas Goodwin's memory:

> In that sermon he [Rogers] falls into an expostulation with the people about their neglect of the Bible: (I am afraid it is more neglected in our days); he personates God to the people, telling them, "Well, I have trusted you so long with my Bible; you have slighted it, it lies in such and such houses all covered with dust and cobwebs; you care not to look into it. Do you use my Bible so? Well, you shall have my Bible no longer."

---

2. Richard Greenham, "A Profitable Treatise, Containing a Discourse for the Reading and Understanding of the Holy Scriptures," in *The Works of the Reverend and Faithfull Servant of Jesus Christ*, M. Richard Greenham, ed. H.[enry] H.[olland] (1599; repr., New York: Da Capo, 1973), 389–97.

3. Henry Smith, "The True Trial of the Spirits," in *The Works of Henry Smith* (Stoke-on-Trent, U.K.: Tentmaker Publications, 2002), 1:141. Cf. Westminster Confession (14.2).

4. Quoted in Charles H. Spurgeon, *The Treasury of David* (Pasadena, Tex.: Pilgrim Publications, 1983), 6:41.

And he takes up the Bible from his cushion, and seemed as if he were going away with it, and carrying it from them; but immediately turns again and personates the people to God, falls down on his knees, cries and pleads most earnestly, "Lord, whatsoever thou dost to us, take not thy Bible from us; kill our children, burn our houses, destroy our goods; only spare us thy Bible, only take not away thy Bible." And then he personates God again to the people: "Say you so? Well, I will try you a little longer; and here is my Bible for you, I will see how you will use it, whether you will love it more, whether you will value it more, whether you will observe it more, whether you will practice it more, and live more according to it." But by these actions…he put all the congregation into so strange a posture that he never saw any congregation in his life. The place was a mere Bochim, the people generally (as it were) deluged with their own tears; and he told me that he himself, when he got out, and was to take horse again to be gone, he was fain to hang a quarter of an hour upon the neck of his horse weeping, before he had power to mount; so strange an impression was there upon him, and generally upon the people, upon having been thus expostulated with for the neglect of the Bible.[5]

The whole story is quite incomprehensible without appreciating that, for the Puritan, the Bible was the most valuable treasure and surest foundation for faith and life that this world affords. In the written Word of God they found the living Word of God, Jesus Christ, revealed as the way, the truth, and the life (John 14:6). Puritanism was all about reforming all of life according to the supremely authoritative standard of the Bible in and through Jesus Christ.

---

5. John Howe, "The Principles of the Oracles of God. In Two Parts," in *The Works of the Rev. John Howe, M.A., Complete in One Volume* (London: Henry G. Bohn, 1846), 1085.

2

The Story of Puritanism

Puritanism was born amid the shock waves of England's Reformation in the sixteenth century. King Henry VIII (reigned 1509–1547) had broken the ties that bound the Church of England to Rome—by the end of his reign, the Church of England was no longer Roman Catholic, that is, no longer in submission to the pope of Rome. But then neither was it really Protestant, at least not in worship or polity. Like Luther, the early Anglicans retained much of pre-Reformation usage in worship, and left the government of their church unchanged, save for acknowledging the monarch as supreme governor.

King Henry's son and successor, Edward VI (reigned 1547–1553), continued to reform the church, making it categorically Protestant. However, Edward's further reformation came to a bone-crunching halt upon his premature death when he was succeeded by his arch-Catholic half sister Mary (reigned 1553–1558). She undid everything, setting the national clock back twenty years to make England once again Roman Catholic. Yet Mary also died prematurely, leaving the throne to her politically astute half sister, Elizabeth (reigned 1558–1603). Elizabeth wanted England to be a united, Protestant nation, and so she settled the Church of England on the foundation of her own peculiarly English idea of Protestantism.

Puritanism's Checkered History in England and New England

All Protestants were delighted to see England recovered from Rome, but those who would soon be called Puritans could never settle for what Elizabeth had established by royal decree. For them it was a church still in need of a good deal more reforming. In Elizabeth's mind, the matter of religion in England was settled almost as soon as she became queen: England was Protestant, the Church of England was as reformed as it had to be, and no more need be said. For the Puritans, on the other hand, the idea of the "Elizabethan settlement" (a position that was primarily but not thoroughly Protestant) stood entirely opposed to a fundamental Protestant conviction, that the visible church must continually be reformed to bring it more and more in line with the Word of God.

So it wasn't just a matter of how things looked or sounded on the Lord's Day. No Puritan could consider the work of reformation complete when the majority of the population still had little or no understanding of justification by faith alone, to say nothing more. It was not enough to reform how the church functioned; the Reformation was also about transforming individual lives, achieving not just an external Protestantism but an internalized, heartfelt faith and life.

After decades of contending with Elizabeth and her ministers, the Puritans began to yearn for the day when her successor, James VI of Scotland, would come to the English throne, subsequently becoming King James I (reigned 1603–1625). He was reared and educated as a Calvinist and a Presbyterian. However, demanding conformity as rigorously as Elizabeth ever had, James was a disappointment for the Puritans of England, and a growing number of Puritans began to separate, some leaving the Church of England, some leaving England itself. And so, in 1620, some eager émigrés set sail for the new world aboard the *Mayflower*. It was a move that would catch the Puritan imagination: the godly fleeing oppression in England looked like Israel fleeing Egypt. And, like Israel, they were seeking a promised land of freedom. There they would establish a New England and build a New Jerusalem. There they would create a fully reformed society, freed from the shackles of the past; it would be "a city on a hill," a beacon to the world. It was a vision so attractive that soon many thousands were following it.

Back in old England, however, things only got worse. James's son Charles I (reigned 1625–1649) began pushing a distinctly anti-Puritan agenda harder and harder. Political and religious tensions mounted until England found herself in a civil war. In God's providence, it was during that tumultuous time that about one hundred Puritan ministers and leaders assembled at Westminster Abbey under Parliament's direction to revise the confession of the national church. In time they decided to draft a new confession of faith to replace the old one. The Westminster Confession, together with the Larger and Shorter Catechisms became doctrinal standards for Puritan theology and remains so for millions of Presbyterians ever since. Meanwhile, Charles I was captured in battle, tried for treason, and executed as a criminal. For a decade, England became a commonwealth under the protectorate of the Cromwells, and a place of unprecedented opportunity for the Puritans.

Yet after a decade the people wanted a king again, and they offered the crown to the son of the king whom they had executed. Under Charles II (reigned 1660–1685) the monarchy was restored. He then took up his father's anti-Puritan agenda with a vengeance. Episcopal church government was reinstated, a revised Prayer Book was imposed, and the clergy were required to declare that it contained nothing contrary to the Word of God and that they would conform to its usage in their churches. A fifth of them—some two thousand pastors—refused and were ejected from their ministries in 1662. Religious assemblies ("conventicles") of more than five persons outside the Church of England were outlawed. Many flouted the law, but persecution grew more intense, and some twenty thousand Puritans were sent to prison over the next twenty years (most famously, John Bunyan, who used his incarceration to write numerous books, including the most famous Puritan classic ever written, *The Pilgrim's Progress*).

The Death of Puritanism

It was soon law that only those who conformed to the Church of England could go to university. This was catastrophic for Puritanism, for the universities at Oxford and Cambridge in particular had been the Puritan seminaries and training grounds. With the next generation hindered from training at these institutions, the number of men of high theological caliber gradually dissipated. Puritanism, after all, had been a movement concerned with words (and most of all, the Word of God), and so when Puritans no longer had easy access to higher education as they once had, the muscle of the movement wasted away.

This loss of academic rigor weakened Puritanism's strong ties to its biblical moorings, so much so that in the years that followed many of their ancestors drifted outside belief in such Christian basics as the Trinity. This, too, was a gradual process: first by division into parties adhering to Independency and immersionism, and then by apostasy from the Reformed faith, lapsing into Arminianism, Unitarianism, and worse as ethics and morality were separated from orthodox doctrine. Justification by faith alone gave way to salvation by good character and good works. Puritanism degenerated into Victorianism, with respectability substituting for godliness.

Because it died such a slow death, it is hard to say definitively when the Puritan era ended. There was no final cataclysm, no last stand. But so many had been ejected, silenced, and suppressed that the old movement found itself ever more scattered and leaderless, until by 1700 or shortly thereafter nobody spoke much of "the Puritans" any more, at least in England. Some have said that Jonathan Edwards (1703–1758) was the last Puritan, but he was born as one out of due time—that is, the movement had already folded.

What is most remarkable, however, is not that Puritanism gradually dissipated but that it lasted as long as it did. When else in church history did a movement of such intense, comprehensive pursuit of holiness last for 150 years?

Perhaps the better question is: How did Puritanism manage to stay vibrant and rather monolithic for such a long period of time?

The Puritan Tradition Lives On

While English Puritanism as a historically definable movement ended, the faith and life of Puritanism continued to be a force in the world. The spirit and influence of Puritanism spread into the rest of the British Isles, particularly among the Scottish and Irish Presbyterians and Covenanters, and then down into the Netherlands, giving birth to the Dutch Further Reformation (*Nadere Reformatie*), and yet further south to influence German Pietism. From Scotland and Ireland, Presbyterianism carried the Westminster Standards to North America beginning in the late seventeenth century, and later, to many other parts of the world.

Later on, the Puritan spirit resurfaced in the Great Awakening in the 1730s and 1740s in a large-scale way. One and a half centuries later, Charles Spurgeon rejected the title accorded to him of *Ultimus Puritanorum* ("The Last of the Puritans") for the simple reason that he spent much of his energy educating and training pastors who might carry on the Puritan tradition, upholding its essential convictions. And in that sense, the story of Puritanism continues today, having undergone a resurgence since the late 1950s with the reprinting of nearly eight hundred Puritan books in the last sixty years, many of which were translated into numerous languages and spread all over the globe. Today the faith and witness of the Puritans is alive and well in the world, though only a comparative few have felt its life-giving power by the Spirit's grace and leading.

3

Puritanism Defined

The foundation of Puritanism was the Bible, but much was built on that foundation. Scholars of the Puritan era have long debated what lies at the heart of Puritanism.

The Essence of Puritanism

The terms *Puritan* and *Puritanism* stuck, though what they meant changed over the years. Some twentieth-century scholars think that the heartbeat of Puritanism is the doctrine of predestination—the teaching that God sovereignly and graciously chooses from eternity His elect people whom He wills to save and justly passes by and rejects the rest of the people in His sovereignty and justice because of their sin.[1] Others think that the main teaching of the Puritans lies in the area of its covenant or federal theology—that is, that God always deals with fallen people through the covenant of grace, declaring His willingness to be their God if they will only live by faith in His Son.[2] Yet others believe that the idea and experience of the conversion of sinners from self-made darkness into God's marvelous light is the essence of Puritanism.[3]

Richard M. Hawkes offers this summary: "Was [English Puritanism] essentially a theological movement, emphasizing covenant theology, predestination, and a reformed church service? Or was the heart of the matter political, asserting the inalienable rights of conscience before God, the rule of natural law over arbitrary prerogative courts, the dependency of the king on parliament, the foundation of state authority in the people? Some modern research has pointed

---

1. William Haller, *The Rise of Puritanism* (New York: Columbia University Press, 1938), 83.
2. Perry Miller, *Errand into the Wilderness* (Cambridge: Belknap Press, 1956), 48–49.
3. Alan Simpson, *Puritanism in Old and New England* (Chicago: University of Chicago Press, 1955), 2.

to a third possibility, that the essence of Puritanism was its piety, a stress on conversion, on existential, heartfelt religion."[4]

Actually, all of these concerns, and more, were involved in Puritanism. Today many scholars and avid readers of Puritan literature have been guilty of reading the Puritans selectively. That is, focusing their attention on some particular aspect or phase of Puritanism, or one's favorite emphasis or theme in Puritan literature. But just as most scholars now agree that John Calvin's teaching cannot be reduced to one central theme since Calvin found all his teachings in the Bible and the Bible has many major themes, so scholars are increasingly coming to the same conclusion about the whole of Puritanism. The essence of Puritan teaching is far too biblical and comprehensive to reduce into one major teaching or doctrine.

Major Puritan Emphases

Standing on the firm foundation of Scripture, Puritan preachers and writers found a wide range of topics and issues to address. Here are a few of the many major issues that Puritan ministers commonly addressed in their sermons and writings:

- The Puritans were passionately committed to focusing on the trinitarian character of Christian theology. They never tired of proclaiming the electing grace of God, the dying love of Jesus Christ, and the applying work of the Holy Spirit in the lives of sinners. Their fascination with Christian experience was not so much motivated by an interest in their experience as it was in the desire to trace out God's saving work within them so that they could render all glory to the triune God—Father, Son, and Holy Spirit.

- In common with the Reformers, the Puritans believed in the centrality of the church in the redemptive work of Christ. They believed that "the acceptable way of worshipping the true God is instituted by Himself." The church's worship should be regulated by His commandments, and "not according to the imaginations or devices of men" (Westminster Confession, 21.1). Consequently, Puritans embraced "the regulative principle of worship," believing that nothing should be added to or subtracted from the Word but that which is displayed in New Testament worship. Puritan minsters focused on plain and earnest preaching, liturgical reform, and church discipline. They believed that there was a polity or order for the

---

4. Richard M. Hawkes, "The Logic of Assurance in English Puritan Theology," *Westminster Theological Journal* 52, no. 2 (Fall 1990): 247.

government of the church revealed in Scripture, and the well-being of the church depended on bringing its life and work into conformity to that order.

- In regard to the individual, the Puritans believed with Paul that a man is justified before God only by faith in Christ, and they focused on personal, comprehensive conversion. They believed with Christ that "except a man be born again, he cannot see the kingdom of God" (John 3:3). So they excelled at preaching the gospel, probing the conscience, awakening the sinner, calling him to repentance and faith, leading him to Christ, and schooling him in the way of Christ. Likewise, the Puritans believed with James that "faith, if it hath not works, is dead, being alone" (James 2:17). So they developed from Scripture a careful description of what a Christian ought to be in his inward life before God, and in all his outward actions and relationships in this life—at home, in the church, at work, and in society. In a phrase, the Puritans were *covenant theologians*. They saw the covenant of grace as a great whole, beginning with the God of the covenant, its outworking in the life of the covenant community, and the work and witness of that community in the world around them.

- In the great questions of national life presented by the crises of their day, the Puritans looked to Scripture for light on the duties, power, and rights of king, Parliament, and citizen-subjects.

Concluding Definition of Puritanism

In this book, the term *Puritan* is used as a combination of all the concerns presented above. Thus, our definition of Puritanism includes not only those who were ejected from the Church of England by the Act of Uniformity in 1662, but also those in England and North America who, from the reign of Elizabeth I until around 1700, worked to reform and purify the church and to lead people toward godly living consistent with the Reformed doctrines of grace.

Peter Lewis rightly says that Puritanism grew out of three needs: (1) the need for biblical preaching and the teaching of sound Reformed doctrine; (2) the need for biblical, personal piety that stresses the work of the Holy Spirit in the faith and life of the believer; and (3) the need to restore biblical simplicity in liturgy, vestments, and church government, so that a well-ordered church life would promote the worship of the triune God as prescribed in His Word.[5]

---

5. Peter Lewis, *The Genius of Puritanism* (Grand Rapids: Soli Deo Gloria, 2011), 11–15.

In summary, then, doctrinally, Puritanism was a kind of vigorous Calvinism; experientially, it was warm and contagious; evangelistically, it was active and urgent, yet tender; ecclesiastically, it was centered on the triune God and His worship and service; politically, it aimed to be scriptural, balanced, and bound by conscience before God in the mutual relations of king, Parliament, and subjects.

Why Puritan Teaching Today?

Can the Puritans teach us anything valuable that we don't already know? Actually, we think they have so much to teach us, that we need to break this down into two chapters. In this chapter, we'll look at a few valuable aspects of their teaching, both positively and negatively, and in the next, at several valuable aspects of their lifestyle.

Learn How to Balance Truth
The Puritans show us how to maintain proper biblical balance in preaching and teaching. Here are two important ways of accomplishing that.

First, by maintaining both the objective and the subjective dimensions of Christianity. The objective is the food for the subjective; thus, the subjective is always rooted in the objective. For example, the Puritans stated that the primary ground of assurance of faith is rooted in the promises of God, but those promises must become increasingly real to the believer through the subjective evidences of grace and the internal witness of the Holy Spirit. Without the Spirit's application, the promises of God lead to self-deceit and carnal presumption. On the other hand, without the promises of God and the illumination of the Spirit, self-examination tends to introspection, spiritual bondage, and legalism. Objective and subjective Christianity, that is, Christianity as truth understood by the mind and believed with the heart, and Christianity as the power of God unto salvation worked out in personal experience, must not be separated from each other.

Second, by maintaining the sovereignty of God and the responsibility of man. Nearly all of the Puritans stressed that God is fully sovereign and man is fully responsible. How that can be resolved logically is beyond our finite minds. When Charles Spurgeon was asked how these two grand, biblical doctrines could be reconciled, he responded as a real heir of the Puritans: "I didn't know that friends needed reconciliation."

He went on to compare these two doctrines to the rails of a track upon which Christianity runs. Just as the rails of a train, which run parallel to each other, appear to merge in the distance, so the doctrines of God's sovereignty and man's responsibility, which seem separate from each other in this life, will merge in eternity. The Puritans would wholeheartedly concur. Our task, they said, is not to force their merging in this life but to keep them in balance and to live accordingly. We must thus strive to believe and live in a way that does justice both to God's sovereignty and to our responsibility in our Christianity.

Learn How to Balance Unity and Controversy

Most Puritans had a clear view of what was of primary importance and what was secondary. When souls hung in the balance, for example, William Perkins (1558–1602), often called "the father of Puritanism," was quick to fight for nonnegotiable truth and to refute error—at times vehemently.

An example of this is his magisterial apologetic piece, *A Reformed Catholick*. During Perkins's career, England's Protestantism was not entirely settled. The country had flip-flopped between Roman Catholic and Protestant monarchs over the course of the previous decades and the populace had not entirely given up Roman superstitions. There were also external threats, including political enemies in league with the Church of Rome and an influx of Jesuit missionaries working as undercover agents to undo the Reformation. Perkins saw the Church of Rome as teaching another religion, one as different from true Christianity as darkness is from light. The future of his beloved country remained uncertain in his estimation. So he took up his pen in an attempt to show the differences in substance between the two religions, in the hope of winning over those yet loyal to the Roman Church, and educating his countrymen.

In balancing unity and controversy, Perkins teaches us two important lessons for today: first, we ought never to abandon the visible church lightly or easily. Second, wherever we choose to draw the line on various doctrines and issues, there should be a clear line between essential and nonessential matters, between those things worth fighting for and those that ought to be tolerated. Perkins is a notable example of striving to find such a line in Scripture and acting accordingly.

Learn How to Live by Faith

Puritan teaching sought to expound the whole gospel for the whole of life. They sought to apply every doctrine they drew from Scripture to practical "uses"—as they expressed it. These "uses" will propel you into passionate, effective action for Christ's kingdom. Their own daily lives integrated Christian truth with covenant vision; they knew no dichotomy between the sacred and the secular.

Their writings can assist you immeasurably in living a life that intentionally, in an integrated fashion, centers on God in every area, appreciating His gifts, and declaring everything "holiness to the Lord."

The Puritans were excellent covenant theologians. They lived covenant theology, covenanting themselves, their families, their churches, and their nation to God. Yet they did not fall into the error of hyper-covenantalism, in which the covenant of grace becomes a substitute for personal conversion. They promoted a comprehensive worldview, a holistic approach of bringing the whole gospel to bear on all of life, striving to bring every action into conformity with Christ, as believers matured and grew in faith. The Puritans wrote on practical subjects such as how to pray, how to develop genuine piety, how to work and play for God's glory, how to conduct family worship, and how to raise children for Christ. In short, they taught how to develop a "rational, resolute, passionate piety [that is] conscientious without becoming obsessive, law-oriented without lapsing into legalism, and expressive of Christian liberty without any shameful lurches into license."[1]

If you would grow in practical Christianity and vital piety, read such Puritan titles as Richard Steele's *The Character of an Upright Man*, George Hamond's *The Case for Family Worship*, Cotton Mather's *Help for Distressed Parents*, and Arthur Hildersham's *Dealing with Sin in Our Children*.

---

1. J. I. Packer, *The Quest for Godliness: The Puritan Vision of the Christian Life* (Wheaton, Ill.: Crossway, 1990), 332–34.

Why the Puritan Lifestyle Today?

Puritan teaching, catechizing, and discipling were greatly strengthened by the exemplary Puritan lifestyle shown by the minister, the parents, and the school teachers, as well as others at home, school, and work. That lifestyle was cultivated through several disciplines of Puritan spirituality which made them "great thinkers, great worshipers, great hopers, and great spiritual warriors."[1] In this chapter, we'll limit ourselves to looking at three aspects of their lifestyle: enduring trials and afflictions, rebuking pride, and living in two worlds at once.

How to Endure Trials

We learn from the Puritans that we need affliction to humble us (Deut. 8:2), to teach us what sin is (Zeph. 1:12), and to bring us to God (Hos. 5:15). As Robert Leighton wrote, "Adversity is the diamond dust heaven polishes its jewels with."[2] The Puritans show us how God's rod of affliction is His means to engrave Christ's image more fully upon us, so that we may be partakers of His righteousness and holiness (Heb. 12:10–11).

If you are presently undergoing trials, read William Bridge's *A Lifting Up for the Downcast*, Thomas Brooks's *A Mute Christian under the Rod*, and Richard Sibbes's *A Bruised Reed*. They will show you how every trial can bring you closer to Christ, teach you to walk by faith, and wean you from this world. As Thomas Watson wrote, "God would have the world hang as a loose tooth which, being easily twitched away, doth not much trouble us."[3] Also, read *The Rare Jewel of Christian Contentment* by Jeremiah Burroughs. It will teach you how to learn contentment through trial. Then, the next time you are buffeted by others, by Satan, or by your own conscience, you will carry those trials to Christ and ask

---

1. Packer, *The Quest for Godliness*, xii.
2. John Blanchard, comp., *The Complete Gathered Gold* (Darlington, England: Evangelical Press, 2006), 650.
3. Thomas Watson, *All Things for Good* (Edinburgh: Banner of Truth, 1986), 29.

Him, by His Spirit, to sanctify you through them so that you may model spiritual contentment for others.

How to Rebuke Pride

The Puritans show us how to subdue pride. They stressed that the Bible teaches us that God hates pride (Prov. 6:16–17). He hates the proud with His heart, curses them with His mouth, and punishes them with His hand (Ps. 119:21; Isa. 2:12; 23:9). Pride was God's first enemy. It was the first sin in paradise and the last we will shed in death. "Pride is the shirt of the soul, put on first and put off last," writes George Swinnock.[4]

As a sin, pride is unique. Other sins turn us away from God, but pride is a direct attack upon God. It lifts our hearts above God and against God, Henry Smith said. Pride seeks to dethrone God and enthrone self.

The Puritans did not consider themselves immune to this sin. Twenty years after his conversion, Jonathan Edwards groaned about the "bottomless, infinite depths of pride" left in his heart. He compared the complexity of pride to an onion—when you pull off one layer, there is always another layer underneath.

The Puritans taught that godly people fight against pride, whereas worldly people feed it. Cotton Mather confessed that when pride filled him with bitterness and confusion before the Lord, "I endeavoured to take a view of my pride as the very image of the Devil, contrary to the image and grace of Christ; as an offense against God, and grieving of His Spirit; as the most unreasonable folly and madness for one who had nothing singularly excellent and who had a nature so corrupt."[5]

How should we fight against pride? The Puritans suggested several strategies. First, consider the huge contrast between a humiliated Christ and a proud Christian. Let's encourage our souls to encamp in Gethsemane and at Calvary, for nowhere is humility cultivated so much as in these two places. Second, seek a deeper knowledge of God, His attributes, and His glory. Job and Isaiah teach us that nothing is so humbling as knowing God and having high, elevated thoughts of Him (Job 42; Isa. 6). Third, meditate much on the solemnity of death, the certainty of Judgment Day, and the vastness of eternity. Fourth, remember daily that "pride goeth before destruction, and an haughty spirit before a fall" (Prov. 16:18). Finally, examine yourself by what the Puritan Richard Mayo said: "Should that

---

4. Cited in I. D. E Thomas, *The Golden Treasury of Puritan Quotations* (Edinburgh: Banner of Truth, 1977), 224.
5. Cited in Charles Bridges, *The Christian Ministry* (London: Banner of Truth, 1959), 152.

man be proud that has sinned as thou hast sinned, and lived as thou hast lived, and wasted so much time, and abused so much mercy, and omitted so many duties, and neglected so great means?—that hath so grieved the Spirit of God, so violated the law of God, so dishonored the name of God? Should that man be proud, who hath such a heart as thou hast?"[6]

How to Live in Dual Worlds

Richard Baxter's *The Saint's Everlasting Rest* shows the power that the hope of heaven has to direct, control, and energize our lives here on earth. Despite its length (800-plus pages), this classic became household reading in Puritan homes. It was surpassed only by John Bunyan's *Pilgrim's Progress*, which is an allegorical outworking of this same truth. Bunyan's pilgrim is heading for the Celestial City, which he never has out of his mind except when he is betrayed by some form of spiritual malaise.

The Puritans believed that we should have heaven "in our eye" throughout our earthly pilgrimage. They took seriously the dual world, now/not-yet dynamics of the New Testament, stressing that keeping the "hope of glory" before our minds should guide and shape our lives here on earth. Living in the light of eternity necessitated radical self-denial. The Puritans taught us to live, knowing that the joy of heaven will more than make amends for any losses and crosses that we must endure on earth as we follow Christ. They taught us that preparation for death by means of sanctified trials lies at the heart of learning to live to God.

---

6. *Puritan Sermons 1659–1689, Being Morning Exercises at Cripplegate* (Wheaton, Ill.: Richard Owen Roberts, 1981), 3:390.

PART TWO

Puritan Stalwarts

William Perkins
(1558–1602)

His Conversion and Education

William Perkins, sometimes called "the father of Puritanism," was born in 1558 to Thomas and Anna Perkins in Warwickshire. As a youth, he indulged in reckless behavior, profanity, and drunkenness. But while a student at Christ's College, Cambridge, Perkins experienced a powerful conversion that began when he overheard a woman in the street chiding her naughty child and alluding to "drunken Perkins." This incident so humiliated Perkins that he gave up his wicked ways and fled to Christ for salvation. He abandoned the study of mathematics and his fascination with black magic and the occult, and took up theology.

To study at Cambridge, the leading Puritan center of the day, meant that Perkins's formal training was shaped by a Calvinistic framework. While studying here, Laurence Chaderton (c. 1536–1640) became his personal tutor and lifelong friend. He and Chaderton met with Richard Greenham (1542–1594), Richard Rogers (1551–1618), and others in a spiritual brotherhood at Cambridge which had a profound influence on young Perkins.

His Ministry

Upon graduating with his master's degree in 1584, Perkins served as "lecturer," or preacher, at Great St. Andrew's Church, Cambridge—a most influential pulpit across the street from Christ's College. He would preach there until his death. He also served as a fellow at Christ's College from 1584 to 1594 where he was responsible to preach, lecture, and mentor students. However, to the distress of others at the College, he resigned from this position to marry a young widow in 1594.

Like his mentor, Chaderton, Perkins worked to purify the established church from within rather than joining Puritans who advocated separation. Instead of addressing questions of church polity, he focused on addressing pastoral inadequacies, spiritual deficiencies, and soul-destroying ignorance in the church.

Perkins had exceptional gifts for expounding the Scriptures and an uncanny ability to reach common people with plain preaching and clearly articulated theology. He aimed to wed predestinarian preaching with practical, godly living. Perkins refused to see the relationship between God's sovereignty and man's responsibility as contradictory but rather as complimentary doctrines that are fully understood in the mind of God, and fully embraced by the converted heart and mind. He also pioneered the practice of Puritan casuistry—the art of dealing with "cases of conscience" by self-examination and scriptural diagnosis. Many people were convicted of sin and delivered from bondage under his preaching.

His Death and Continuing Influence
Perkins died from kidney stone complications in 1602, just before the end of Queen Elizabeth's reign. By the time of his death, Perkins's writings in England were outselling those of Calvin, Beza, and Bullinger combined. Thomas Goodwin (1600–1680) wrote that when he entered Cambridge ten years later, six of his instructors who had sat under Perkins were still passing on his teaching and that Cambridge was filled with the power of his preaching.

As a rhetorician, expositor, theologian, and pastor, Perkins became the principle architect of the Puritan movement. His vision of reform for the church, combined with his intellect, piety, writing, spiritual counseling, and communication skills, enabled him to set the tone for the seventeenth-century Puritan accent on Reformed, experiential truth and self-examination, and Puritan polemic against Roman Catholicism and Arminianism.

Recommended Books
The Works of William Perkins (10 vols., Reformation Heritage Books), which includes volumes 1–4 of exegetical works, including *Sermon on the Mount: Matthew 5–7, Commentary on Galatians, Commentary on Hebrews 11, Exposition of Jude,* and *Revelation 1–3;* volumes 5–7 of doctrinal and polemical works, including expositions of *The Lord's Prayer* and *The Apostles' Creed, Foundation of the Christian Religion, The Manner and Order of Predestination,* and *Reformed Catholic;* and volumes 8–10 of practical works, including *Discourse of Conscience, The Nature and Practice of Repentance, A Treatise on How to Live Well in All Estates, A Treatise on Vocations,* and *The Right Manner of Erecting and Ordering a Family. The Art of Prophesying*—a classic on the basics of preaching. *The Golden Chain of Salvation*—focuses on God's way of salvation.

Richard Sibbes
(1577–1635)

His Early Years and Conversion

Richard Sibbes was born in 1577 at Tostock, Suffolk, in the heartland of English Puritanism. He was baptized in the parish church in Thurston and went to school there. As a child he loved books. His father, Paul Sibbes, a hardworking wheelwright (a maker and repairer of wooden wheels) and godly Christian man, became irritated with his son's interest in books. He tried to cure his son of book-buying by offering him wheelwright tools, but the boy was not to be dissuaded.

With the support of others, Sibbes was admitted to St. John's College, Cambridge, at the age of eighteen. He received a bachelor of arts degree in 1599, a fellowship in 1601, and a master of arts degree in 1602. In 1603, he was converted under the preaching of Paul Baynes, whom Sibbes called his "father in the gospel."

His Ministry

Sibbes was ordained to the ministry in the Church of England in Norwich in 1608. He was chosen as one of the college preachers in 1609. From 1611 to 1616, he served as lecturer at Holy Trinity Church, Cambridge. His preaching awakened Cambridge from the spiritual indifference into which it had fallen after the death of Perkins.

Sibbes came to London in 1617 as a lecturer for Gray's Inn, the largest of the four Inns of Court, the professional associations or communities to which all barristers (lawyers) belonged, each of which had a church connected with it. In 1626, he also became master of St. Catharine's College, Cambridge. Under his leadership, the college regained some of its former prestige. Soon after his appointment, Sibbes received the doctor of divinity degree at Cambridge. He became known as "the heavenly Doctor" due to his godly preaching and heavenly-minded manner of life. In 1633, King Charles I offered Sibbes the charge of Holy Trinity, Cambridge. Sibbes continued to serve as preacher at Gray's Inn, master of St. Catherine's Hall, and vicar of Holy Trinity until his death in 1635.

Puritans everywhere recognized Sibbes as a Christ-centered, experiential preacher and divine. Sibbes wrote, "To preach is to woo. The main scope of all [preaching] is, to allure us to the entertainment of Christ's mild, safe, wise, victorious government."[1] Both learned and unlearned in upper and lower classes profited greatly from Sibbes's alluring preaching. The twentieth-century historian William Haller said Sibbes's sermons were "the most brilliant and popular of all the utterances of the Puritan church militant."[2]

His Death and Continuing Influence

Sibbes's last sermons, preached a week before his death, were on John 14:2, "In my Father's house are many mansions.... I go to prepare a place for you." When asked in his final days how his soul was faring, Sibbes replied, "I should do God much wrong if I should not say, very well." Sibbes went to be with his gracious Savior on July 5, 1635.

Subsequent to his death, his writings continued to have a profound influence and were cherished among God's people. David Masson, biographer of John Milton, wrote, "No writings in practical theology seem to have been so much read in the mid-seventeenth century among the pious English middle classes as those of Sibbes."[3]

Recommended Books

The Works of Richard Sibbes (7 vols.)—includes several frequently reprinted works, such as *The Bruised Reed* (vol. 1), *The Returning Backslider* (vol. 2), *Glorious Freedom* (vol. 2), *The Fountain Sealed* and *The Fountain Opened* (vol. 5).

---

1. Richard Sibbes, "The Fountain Opened," in *The Works of Richard Sibbes*, ed. Alexander Grosart (Edinburgh: Banner of Truth, 1973), 5:505.
2. Cited in Joel R. Beeke and Randall J. Pedersen, *Meet the Puritans* (Grand Rapids: Reformation Heritage Books, 2006), 536.
3. Cited in Beeke and Pederson, *Meet the Puritans*, 536.

8

Thomas Goodwin
(1600–1680)

His Childhood and Education

Thomas Goodwin was born October 5, 1600, in Rollesby, England. His God-fearing parents, Richard and Katherine Goodwin, did their best to train their son for the ministry through their personal example as well as by providing him with the best classical education offered by local schools. As a child, Goodwin possessed a tender conscience and experienced vivid impressions of God and eternity.

By age thirteen, he was enrolled at Christ's College, Cambridge. Though surrounded by Puritan preaching and teaching, Goodwin set his heart on becoming a popular preacher, focusing on the study of rhetoric and embracing Arminianism.

Goodwin graduated from Christ's College with a bachelor's degree in 1617. In 1619, he continued his studies at St. Catharine's Hall in Cambridge, graduating with a master's degree and becoming a fellow and lecturer a year later.

His Conversion and Early Ministry

Providentially, Goodwin was challenged by other fellows at Cambridge who sought to persuade him of the folly of empty rhetoric and Arminianism. In addition, he could not shake off the influence of the pointed gospel preaching of Richard Sibbes and John Preston in the college chapel. On October 2, 1620, upon hearing a funeral sermon on Luke 19:41–42, God brought Goodwin under profound conviction of sin and he was converted. He began to align himself with the theological tradition of the Puritans and his preaching became earnest, experiential, and pastoral.

In 1625, Goodwin was licensed as a preacher. By 1628, he was appointed lecturer at Trinity Church, succeeding Sibbes and Preston at age twenty-seven. He served there until the end of 1633, being forced to resign due to his unwillingness to submit to Archbishop Laud's articles of conformity.

He began serving as a Separatist preacher in London but because of increasing restrictions against preaching, Goodwin took refuge in the Netherlands in

1639. He worked in Arnhem, serving more than a hundred people who had fled from Laud's persecution.

His Later Ministry and Death

In 1641, after Laud was impeached, Goodwin responded to Parliament's invitation to return to England. He was appointed as a member of the Westminster Assembly, where he played a very prominent role.

After the assembly recessed, Goodwin was appointed as a lecturer at Oxford and then became president of Magdalen College. Goodwin helped shape this institution according to scriptural truth and experiential Calvinistic doctrine. He demanded such academic excellence and dealt so plainly with the spiritual lives of the students that he was accused of operating a "scruple shop" by those who did not appreciate his Puritan emphases. During this time he also served as a chaplain to Cromwell and organized an Independent church.

On September 29, 1658, Goodwin, along with a number of well-known Independent pastors and theologians, drew up the Savoy Declaration of Faith and Order, a redacted version of the Westminster Confession of Faith. This document became the confessional standard for British Congregationalism and was later adopted by American Congregationalists.

With the accession of Charles II in 1660 and the accompanying loss of Puritan public influence, Goodwin felt compelled to leave Oxford. He and most of his Independent congregation moved to London, where they made a new start as a church. Goodwin devoted his last years to preaching, pastoral work, and writing, dying at age eighty.

Recommended Books

The Works of Thomas Goodwin (12 vols.)—includes numerous classic works, such as *A Child of Light Walking in Darkness* and *The Vanity of Thoughts* (vol. 3), *Christ Set Forth* and *The Heart of Christ in Heaven towards Sinners on Earth* (vol. 4), *Christ the Mediator* (vol. 5), *The Work of the Holy Spirit* (vol. 6), *The Object and Acts of Justifying Faith* (vol. 8), *A Discourse of Election* (vol. 9), and *An Unregenerate Man's Guiltiness before God* (vol. 10).

9

John Eliot
(1604–1690)

His Early Years

John Eliot, known as the Apostle to the Indians, was born to a wealthy family in England in 1604. As a boy, he enjoyed studying and went to Jesus College, Cambridge, in 1619, where he earned a bachelor of arts degree in 1622. Upon graduation, he was ordained in the Church of England, but he was soon dissatisfied with its rules and usages. Instead of searching for a sympathetic parish, he chose to teach at the grammar school in Essex, where Thomas Hooker was master. Under Hooker's influence, Eliot came to faith in Christ. Soon after his conversion, Eliot felt called to devote himself to the ministry.

With the closing of Hooker's school and increasing pressures for conformity, Eliot decided to immigrate to Massachusetts. He arrived in Boston on November 3, 1631. He settled in Roxbury, Massachusetts, serving the church there as teacher and later as pastor for more than fifty years. The first fifteen years he devoted himself wholly to the work of the church; during the next thirty-five he divided his time between pastoring the congregation and working among Native Americans. Eliot became widely known as a skilled preacher and counselor.

His Ministry to the Massachusett Tribe

After studying the Algonquian language for a few years, Eliot began preaching to the natives in 1646. Under the blessing of God, Eliot began to set up towns of "praying Indians." By 1674, there were fourteen "praying towns" with an estimated population of 3,600; approximately 1,100 showed fruits of having been converted. In each town, the natives made a solemn covenant to give themselves and their children "to God to be His people" as the basis of their new civil government. These towns were almost entirely self-governing. For the most part, the natives were expected to adopt the Puritan lifestyle along with the Christian faith.

After organizing the civil government, Eliot started establishing Indian churches with a Congregationalist form of government. Having overcome numerous difficulties in a fifteen-year period, the first native church was officially established in 1660, with others to follow soon after.

Throughout this time, Eliot had been laboring to translate the Bible into Algonquian, the language of the original inhabitants of the Bay State. With the help of English supporters, he established a printing press where the first New Testament in the Massachusett language was printed in 1661. The Old Testament with a version of the Psalms in meter followed in 1663, making it the first complete Bible printed on the American continent. The Algonquian Bible is considered by many to be Eliot's greatest accomplishment, but for Eliot, that Bible was simply an aid to the conversion of Native Americans.

His Later Years
Eliot's work prospered until the onset of King Philip's War in 1675. Fearing for their lives, numerous native converts moved to an island in Boston harbor. Many died there. That pattern was repeated in other towns, where praying Indians were destroyed by either warring tribesmen or vengeful colonists. In the end, the fourteen praying towns were wiped out. Eliot attempted to start over after the war, but despite his efforts, these towns were never recovered.

In his final years, Eliot was consumed with a passion for Christ and his beloved Native Americans. He died May 20, 1690, at the age of eighty-six. His last words were, "Welcome joy!"

Recommended Books
The Eliot Tracts—a collection that contains the complete set of eleven tracts written by leaders among the colonists (including Eliot and Thomas Shepard), which offer the most detailed record of missionary activity by the English in the New World.

The Indian Grammar Begun—Eliot's grammar that was designed to promote the gospel among Native Americans.

10

John Owen
(1616–1683)

His Early Years

John Owen, called the "prince of the English divines," was born in Stadham, England, to Henry Owen, the local Puritan vicar. Owen showed godly and scholarly tendencies at an early age. He entered Queen's College, Oxford, at the age of twelve, earning his bachelor of arts degree in 1632 and a master of arts degree in 1635. Throughout his teenage years, young Owen studied eighteen to twenty hours per day.

Owen left Oxford in 1637 and became a private chaplain and tutor. These years of chaplaincy afforded him much time for study, which God richly blessed. At the age of twenty-six, Owen began a forty-one year writing career that produced more than eighty books.

Though he embraced Puritan convictions from his youth, Owen lacked personal assurance of faith until he heard a sermon preached in 1642 on the text, "Why are ye fearful, O ye of little faith?" (Matt. 8:26). God powerfully used that sermon to bring Owen to assurance of faith.

His Years of Prominence

In 1643, Owen published *A Display of Arminianism*, a vigorous exposition and defense of Calvinism. This book earned Owen nearly instant recognition as well as an appointment to the pastorate in Fordham. His ministry was well-received there, and many people came from outlying districts to hear him. He excelled, not only in preaching, but also in catechizing his parishioners.

Being removed from that position for political reasons, Owen became vicar of the distinguished Essex pulpit of St. Peter's, Coggeshall, in 1646. Here he openly converted from Presbyterianism to Congregationalism, restructuring his congregation after Congregational principles. Owen's fame spread rapidly in the late 1640s through his preaching and writings, gradually earning him a reputation as a leading Independent theologian.

Oliver Cromwell, impressed by a sermon that Owen preached before Parliament, persuaded Owen to accompany him as chaplain to Ireland to regulate the affairs of Trinity College in Dublin. He spent most of his time there reorganizing the college along Puritan lines, as well as preaching.

In 1650, Owen was appointed as an official preacher to the commonwealth. This decade would prove to be Owen's most productive years. In 1651, he became dean of Christ Church College, Oxford, and eighteen months later was made vice-chancellor of Oxford University. Through his lectures in theology and his numerous publications, he promoted Reformed theology and Puritan piety. Owen's godly leadership brought peace, stability, and spiritual growth to the university during the difficult period of recovery from the chaotic civil war years.

His Years of Relative Obscurity

After Cromwell was succeeded by his son Richard, Owen and others lost their ecclesiastical positions to Presbyterian divines. In 1660, Owen was replaced as dean of Christ Church by Edward Reynolds. He retired to his small estate at Stadham, where he continued to preach. In 1665, he started a small congregation in London where he served and continued to write. In 1673, this congregation merged with a church where Joseph Caryl had served as pastor.

Owen suffered much from asthma and gallstones in his last years, both of which often kept him from preaching. He kept writing, however, producing major works on justification, spiritual-mindedness, and the glory of Christ. Owen died on August 24, 1683, full of joyous expectation for the glory to come.

Recommended Books

The Works of John Owen (16 vols.)—divided into three major sections: doctrinal (vols. 1–5), practical (vols. 6–9), and polemical (vols. 10–16)—the most renowned being *The Person and Glory of Christ* (vol. 1), *Communion with God* (vol. 2), *Discourse on the Holy Spirit* (vol. 3), *Justification by Faith* (vol. 5), *Mortification of Sin, Temptation*, and *Exposition of Psalm 130* (vol. 6), *Spiritual Mindedness* (vol. 7), *The Death of Death in the Death of Christ* (vol. 10), and *The Doctrine of the Saints' Perseverance* (vol. 11).

An Exposition of the Epistle to the Hebrews (7 vols.)—the definitive commentary on Hebrews throughout the centuries since its publication.

11

John Bunyan
(1628–1688)

His Conversion

John Bunyan was born in 1628 at Elstow, near Bedford, to Thomas Bunyan and Margaret Bentley. Growing up in a poor family, John did not receive a good education. He was lawless and rebellious, frequently indulging in cursing and blasphemy. Sporadic periods of conviction of sin, however, helped restrain some of that disobedience.

When Bunyan was sixteen years old, he joined Cromwell's New Model Army, where he continued his rebellious ways. However, fighting in the English Civil War sobered him considerably, especially after a near-death experience. Bunyan was discharged from the army in 1646 or 1647.

In 1648, Bunyan married a God-fearing woman whose name remains unknown. After reading her Puritan literature, he was once more convicted of sin. He started attending the parish church, stopped swearing, and tried to honor the Lord's Day. After some months, Bunyan came into contact with some women whose joyous conversation about Christ and the new birth deeply impressed him. He mourned his joyless existence as he realized that he was lost and outside of Christ. He felt that he had the worst heart in all of England.

In 1651, the women introduced Bunyan to John Gifford, their pastor in Bedford. God used Gifford to lead Bunyan to repentance and faith. In 1655, he moved to Bedford with his wife and four children, became a member of Gifford's church, and was soon appointed deacon. His testimony became the talk of the town and led several people to conversion.

His Early Ministry and Imprisonment

In 1655, Bunyan began preaching to various congregations in Bedford. Hundreds came to hear him. Over the next few years he would publish a number of books, establishing himself as a reputable Puritan writer.

In early 1661, Bunyan was arrested on the charge of preaching without official license from the crown. When told that he would be freed if he would no longer preach, he replied, "If I am freed today, I will preach tomorrow." Bunyan remained in prison for twelve and a half years with no formal charge and no legal sentence because he refused to give up preaching the gospel and denounced the Church of England as false. In 1661 and from 1668–1672, however, certain jailers permitted Bunyan to leave prison at times to preach.

His prison years were times of difficult trials, especially the pain of separation from his wife and children. These years, however, were productive years for Bunyan. He wrote tirelessly and prolifically, producing many of the dozens of his books, several of which became classics.

His Later Ministry and Imprisonment
In May of 1672, he was released to pastor the Bedford congregation. After enjoying freedom for a couple of years, he was once more arrested for preaching and put in the town jail again. Here he wrote many works, including the first part of his famous *Pilgrim's Progress*. Being released in 1677, he spent his last years preaching and writing.

In 1688, Bunyan died suddenly from a fever that he caught while traveling in cold weather. On his death bed, having told his friends that his greatest desire was to be with Christ, he raised his hands to heaven, and cried, "Take me, for I come to Thee!" and then died.

Recommended Books
The Pilgrim's Progress—a moving, allegorical account of spiritual warfare experienced by a wayfaring pilgrim named Christian traveling from this world to heaven—a must read that became the bestseller of the thousands of Puritan titles, for both adults and children.

Grace Abounding to the Chief of Sinners—an autobiographical classic that chronicles Bunyan's life from infancy to his imprisonment in 1660.

12

John Flavel
(1628–1691)

His Early Years

John Flavel was born in 1628 in Bromsgrove, Worcestershire. He was the son of Richard Flavel, a Nonconformist minister. John was educated by his father in the ways of religion, going on to study at University College, Oxford. In 1650, he was ordained by the presbytery at Salisbury. He settled in Diptford, where he honed his numerous gifts.

He married Joan Randall, a godly woman, who died while giving birth to their first child in 1655. The baby died as well. After a year of mourning, Flavel married Elizabeth Stapell and was again blessed with a close, God-fearing marriage, as well as several children.

In 1656, Flavel accepted a call to be minister in the thriving seaport town of Dartmouth. This position earned a smaller income than he had received in Diptford, but his work was more profitable. Many were converted through his ministry here.

His Turbulent, Yet Fruitful Ministry

Flavel was ejected from the pulpit in 1662 for nonconformity but continued to meet secretly with his parishioners for worship. Once he even disguised himself as a woman on horseback in order to reach a secret meeting place where he preached and administered baptism. At another time, when pursued by authorities, he plunged his horse into the sea and managed to escape arrest by swimming through a rocky area to reach safety.

In 1665, Flavel moved to Slapton were he continued to minister to many people in his congregation. At times, he would preach secretly in the woods to large numbers of people, sometimes until midnight. On one such occasion, soldiers rushed in and dispersed the congregation. Several of the fugitives were apprehended and fined, but the remainder brought Flavel to another wooded area where he continued his sermon.

In 1672, King Charles II issued the Declaration of Indulgence, giving Non-conformists freedom to worship. Flavel returned to Dartmouth, licensed as a Congregationalist. When the indulgence was canceled the following year, Flavel once more resorted to preaching secretly in private homes, secluded neighborhoods, or remote forests.

Flavel's second wife died during this time and he married Ann Downe, a minister's daughter. They were happily married for eleven years and had two sons.

In the late 1670s and early 1680s, Flavel carried on his ministry mainly by writing. He published at least nine books in this period. But in the summer of 1682 he was forced to seek safety in London, where he assisted in a friend's congregation. While there, Flavel's third wife died.

His Final Years

Having married a fourth time, Flavel returned to Dartmouth in 1684, where, under house arrest, his ministry was confined to his home. There he preached every Sunday and on many weekday evenings to the gathered crowds, even in the face of official antagonism.

In 1687, King James II issued another indulgence for Nonconformists that allowed Flavel to preach publicly once again. His congregation built a large chapel to herald his return to the pulpit. His last four years of public preaching were greatly blessed. Yet his health was declining rapidly. While visiting Exeter to preach in June of 1691, Flavel suffered a massive stroke and died that same evening at the age of sixty-three. His final words were, "I know that it will be well with me."

Recommended Books

The Works of John Flavel (6 vols.), which contain several classic volumes, including *The Mystery of Providence* (probably the best book ever written on the subject); *Christ Knocking at the Door of the Heart* (eleven sermons on Rev. 3:20); *The Fountain of Life* (forty-two sermons on the riches of Christ's offices and states); *Keeping the Heart* (six ways to keep your heart before God, which is the great calling of every believer); and *The Method of Grace* (a detailed description of the Spirit's work in applying Christ's redemption to sinners).

13

Matthew Henry
(1662–1714)

His Childhood and Education

Matthew Henry was born at Broad Oak, Flintshire, in England on October 18, 1662, less than two months after his father, Philip Henry, was ejected from the ministry of the Church of England. Born prematurely, he was a frail child yet was spiritually robust and intellectually gifted. He was educated primarily by his father, with the assistance of tutors.

Henry entered Thomas Doolittle's academy at Islington in 1680. He studied there under Doolittle and Thomas Vincent for two years; then, when persecution forced the academy to relocate, Henry returned to Flintshire. Realizing his chances of being called to the ministry were remote, Henry decided to enter the legal profession. He was admitted to Gray's Inn in 1685 to study law, while continuing theological study in private.

His Ministry in Chester

In 1686, Henry began to preach in his father's neighborhood. Because of business matters, he moved to Chester in 1687. He preached there in private houses until he was asked to become the local minister. On May 9, 1687, he was privately ordained in London and began ministering in Chester. Within a few years, the number of communicants in his congregation grew to 250.

In 1687, Henry married Katherine Hardware, but she died in childbirth only two years later. In 1690, Henry married Mary Warburton. They had one son, Philip, and eight daughters, three of whom died in infancy.

A meetinghouse built for Henry in Crook Lane was opened in 1700. In 1706, a gallery was added to accommodate another congregation that joined Henry's, raising the number of communicants to 350. In addition to his congregational work, Henry held monthly services at five neighboring villages and regularly preached to prisoners in the castle.

In 1704, at the age of forty-two, Henry began work on a Bible commentary based on his system of expository preaching and the copious notes and writings on the Bible compiled during his ministry. He had learned Hebrew, Greek, and Latin as a child, and also had a working knowledge of French. Additionally, he had a keen spirit of inquiry and the ability to express doctrinal matters in a simple yet profound way.

His Ministry in London

In 1710, Henry was invited to Hackney, one of the most important Nonconformist congregations near London. He agreed to move, though not immediately. He preached his farewell sermon at Chester on May 11, 1712, amid many tears. His ministry at Mare Street, Hackney, began the following week, but would be short-lived. In June of 1714, while returning to London, he fell from his horse and died the following day.

Though Matthew Henry is most remembered for his commentary on the Bible, he wrote thirty additional works, focusing primarily on practical godliness. The message of Henry's life and ministry was simple: "A life spent in the service of God, and communion with him, is the most comfortable life anyone can live in this world."

Recommended Books

Commentary on the Whole Bible (6 vols.)—the most valuable, popular commentary ever written.

Complete Works of Matthew Henry (2 vols.)—includes numerous valuable books written by Henry (excluding his commentary), such as *The Covenant of Grace, How to Prepare for Communion, A Method for Prayer, The Pleasantness of a Religious Life*, and *The Secret of Communion with God*.

14

Jonathan Edwards
(1703–1758)

His Childhood and Education

Jonathan Edwards was born October 5, 1703, in East Windsor, Connecticut. Edwards's father and maternal grandfather were both powerful preachers and no strangers to religious revivals. Edwards received his early education in his father's grammar school, where he was nurtured and instructed in Reformed theology and Puritan piety.

At age thirteen, he went on to the Collegiate School (later known as Yale College). He was awarded a bachelor of arts degree in 1720, finishing at the top of his class, and then stayed on at Yale to study for a master's degree. Edwards experienced several periods of spiritual conviction in his childhood and youth, which culminated in his conversion in 1721.

His Early Ministry

Edwards's ministerial career began in 1722 when invited to minister at a Presbyterian church in New York City. This pastorate was short-lived, however, for Edwards was persuaded by his father to return to Connecticut only eight months later. Finishing his master's degree at Yale, he took a call to the parish church at Bolton in November 1723.

The following year, Edwards returned to New Haven to serve as tutor at the college. Edwards remained there until 1726, when he received a summons from the people of Northampton, Massachusetts, to serve as assistant to his aged grandfather, Solomon Stoddard. He was installed there on February 15, 1727 and became sole minister of the parish church upon the death of Stoddard in 1729.

Edwards faced the problem of promoting godliness in a congregation that seemed to be falling into spiritual indifference. Consequently, he focused his preaching in the early 1730s on common, specific sins, urging the people to repent and to embrace the gospel by faith. By the Spirit's grace, his preaching prompted a significant awakening at Northampton in the winter of 1734–1735.

After a lull in the late 1730s, Edwards was caught up in the Great Awakening, which began in 1740; he became one of the ablest instruments and defenders of the revival. He wrote many works in its defense, the most influential being his *Treatise Concerning Religious Affections*.

His Later Ministry

Due to his refusal to baptize infants of members who could not profess saving grace, along with false rumors spreading about his treatment of some young people and complications resulting from several discipline cases, the members of the Northampton church voted to eject Edwards from the pulpit in June 1750. The following year, Edwards left Northampton with his family, taking refuge in the frontier settlement of Stockbridge, where he served as pastor to a small congregation and a missionary to the Housatonic Indians. Though Edwards's desire to witness revival among the Indians did not materialize, these were his most fruitful years, producing a vast body of his writings.

In 1758, Edwards agreed to become president of the College of New Jersey at Princeton. On March 22, 1758, after only a few months at Princeton, he died of complications from a smallpox inoculation. His vast array of writings continue to be mined, pondered, and evaluated to the present day, evidencing him to be, as some view it, America's last Puritan and finest theologian.

Recommended Books

The Works of Jonathan Edwards (2 vols., Banner of Truth; 26 vols., Yale) contains Edwards's greatest classics, among which are *Narrative of Surprising Conversions, A History of the Work of Redemption, Justification by Faith Alone,* and *Charity and Its Fruits*, as well as his more challenging classics to read: *The Freedom of the Will* and *Original Sin Defended*.

The Religious Affections—often regarded as the leading classic in America history on spiritual life.

The Life and Diary of David Brainerd—a moving spiritual classic on par with Augustine's *Confessions*, revealing the spiritual growth and intense struggles of a young missionary zealous for God.

PART THREE

The Triune God and His Saving Work

15

Communion with the Triune God

John Owen's *Communion with God* (1657) stands out among the many great works of Puritan devotional theology. Essentially it is a summons for Christians to be Trinitarian in practice as well as in faith, and it captures Owen's passion for a theology both resolutely Trinitarian and thoroughly applied.

Owen was emphatic that it is quite impossible for anyone ever to have anything to do with "God" in general, simply put. There is no undifferentiated Godhead for any to deal with. We must say with Article 3 of the Athanasian Creed: "We worship one God in Trinity, and Trinity in Unity, neither confounding the Persons nor dividing the Substance." Each person of the Trinity is inseparable from the others, but they are *distinct*, and Owen wanted to show how we can have distinct communion with each person. He bases his case on numerous texts, but most of all on the Apostolic Benediction of 2 Corinthians 13:14: "The grace of the Lord Jesus Christ, and the love of God, and the communion of the Holy Ghost, be with you all."

Communion with the Father
The essence of the Father's communion with us, Owen says, is *love*. Owen was acutely aware that we easily think of the Father, not as loving, but as stern and thunderous in His transcendental distance from us. We conceive of the Father as only being compassionate and tender toward us by the blood of Jesus. Yet in fact, Owen observes, the Father is the very origin and fountain of love: He is the one who in love sent His Son into the world. So, concerning the heavenly Father, who is the fountainhead of all, including the love of God, Owen directs us to:

> Sit down a little at the fountain, and you will quickly have a farther discovery of the sweetness of the streams. You who have run from him, will not be able, after a while, to keep at a distance for a moment.[1]

---

1. John Owen, *Of Communion with God*, in *The Works of John Owen*, ed. William Goold, 16 vols. (Edinburgh: Banner of Truth, 1965–1968), 2:36.

What is this love of the Father? Owen says that it is, first, a "love of complacency," that is, a love that takes pleasure in its objects. God the Father is joyously, delightedly content in and with His children (Zeph. 1:17). Second, God the Father loves His children in Christ, for Christ is "the *treasury* wherein the Father disposeth all the riches of his grace, taken from the bottomless mine of his eternal love; and he is the priest into whose hand we put all the offerings that we return unto the Father."[2] Third, the Father's love is abundant—"the love of a spring, of a fountain—always communicating."[3] Fourth, the Father's love precedes the returning love of the saints. The Father loves His children prior to their loving Him. Finally, the Father's love is steady, whether believers have a sense of it or not; His love never diminishes, falters, or fails.[4]

Communion with the Son

The next section of Owen's treatise is devoted to the Son's communion with us as believers, the essence of which is *grace*. Here Owen suffuses the pages with the language and imagery of the Song of Solomon. Understanding it to be a parable of the love between Christ and His bride, the church, Owen keeps returning to it so as to make readers feel the sweetness of communion with the Son both in His person and through His purchase of them by His blood.

Owen starts by looking at some of "the personal excellencies of the Lord Christ," for it is by appreciating them that our hearts will warm to Him. Christ is shown to the reader to be so irresistibly attractive that our hearts are drawn to Him. More, He is not only beautiful and desirable in Himself, He delights in those who believe in Him and gives Himself over entirely to love for them. Thus, He causes them to delight in Him and give themselves over in love to Him.

Next, Owen moves on to what the Son has done for us. Strikingly, Owen expounds a characteristically Puritan belief, that Christ, in His life, death, resurrection, and ascension, is a mediator who brings us to a profound enjoyment of God.

Communion with the Spirit

Lastly, Owen addresses the Spirit's communion with us, the essence of which is *comfort*. The Spirit, Owen argues, is essentially the Spirit of sanctification. That means, first, that He sets people apart by giving them new birth and works faith

---

2. Owen, *Of Communion with God*, in *Works*, 2:27.
3. Owen, *Of Communion with God*, in *Works*, 2:28.
4. Owen, *Of Communion with God*, in *Works*, 2:29–30.

in their hearts by the preaching of the gospel; and second, He then comforts those who have been set apart from the world by their faith in Christ. By "comfort" Owen is referring to the comfort found only in Christ, which is the only comfort the Spirit affords, by applying to believers what they have in Christ.

That is to say, the Spirit makes communion with the Son and the Father both real and delightful, shedding abroad the love of God and confirming the truth of the gospel in our hearts. Whereas Satan comes to rob us of confidence and comfort, the Spirit brings assurance and enjoyment of the truth. And only the Spirit can do that. When on earth, Owen notes, Christ seemed to affect the hearts of His disciples so little, but when the Spirit came, their hearts were all aflame for Christ and God. Owen concludes: "And this is his work to the end of the world—to bring the promises of Christ to our minds and hearts, to give us the comfort of them, the joy and sweetness of them."[5]

All that said, Owen is aware that some readers may view the Spirit as a mere impersonal divine force. So he is emphatic that, while the Spirit is sent out of the Father's love to communicate the Son's grace, the Spirit still comes of His own will. He is a real person, and can and must be related to as such: "The Holy Ghost, being God, is no less to be invocated, prayed to, and called on, than the Father and Son."[6] Thus, though He will never leave the elect, He may at times withdraw the sense of His comfort, if, for example, they grieve or resist Him.

Conclusion

Owen's conclusion is powerfully Trinitarian:

> The emanation of divine love to us begins with the Father, is carried on by the Son, and then communicated by the Spirit; the Father designing, the Son purchasing, the Spirit effectually working: which is their order. Our participation is first by the work of the Spirit, to an actual interest in the blood of the Son; whence we have acceptation with the Father.[7]

Owen built a powerful case for being Trinitarian in faith and practice. On any other terms, there is a destructive and impoverishing tendency in both theology and worship to reduce all the great particular truths of the gospel to a generalized, empty theism and a powerless, idealistic moralism, devoid of the fullness of truth and life found in God's Word.

---

5. Owen, *Of Communion with God*, in *Works*, 2:237.
6. Owen, *Of Communion with God*, in *Works*, 2:229–30.
7. Owen, *Of Communion with God*, in *Works*, 2:180.

16

God the Father:
Predestination, Creation, and Providence

The Puritans started all their theology with a blessed view of God. The living God, they saw, lacks for nothing, and is all-sufficient in Himself. And it is from that fullness of God that all the goodness of the gospel flows. Richard Sibbes wrote,

> The Father, Son, and Holy Ghost were happy in themselves, and enjoyed one another before the world was. But that God delights to communicate and spread his goodness, there had never been a creation nor a redemption. God useth his creatures, not for defect of power, that he can do nothing without them, but for the spreading of his goodness.... Such a goodness is in God as is in a fountain, or in the breast that loves to ease itself of milk.[1]

In other words, behind all things the Puritans saw a glorious God of love and abundance: Father, Son, and Holy Spirit living in mutual and eternal love and communion. God did not need to create the world in order to satisfy any need He felt or in order to be Himself. The divine majesty of this God is not dependent on the world or anything else outside of Himself.

God Sovereignly Plans

But the Father so enjoyed His fellowship with His Son that His love for Him overflowed and He decreed that the eternal Son should be the firstborn among many sons. As the apostle Paul puts it in Romans 8:29, "For whom he did foreknow, he also did predestinate to be conformed to the image of his Son, that he might be the firstborn among many brethren" (see also Eph. 1:3–5). By His grace, in Christ, mere creatures would be brought to know, call upon, and glorify God "by the sweet name of Father."[2]

Thus the Puritans saw that the history and workings of the universe—of both creation and redemption—are not built on shaky or shifting foundations

---

1. Sibbes, "The Successful Seeker," in *Works*, 6:113.
2. Sibbes, "The Matchless Love and Inbeing," in *Works*, 6:386.

or conditions. God is the author. The existence and history of creation and the unfolding plan of redemption are all founded directly upon nothing less than the immutable perfection of God's will.

The Puritans, like the Reformers before them, agreed—based on Romans 9–11—that this eternal plan of God included predestination, which has two aspects: (1) the election to everlasting life of those whom the Father determined to love in Christ from eternity past to eternity future, for no reason in them, but only out of His sovereign and free grace, and (2) the reprobation of those whom the Father determined to pass by from eternity past to eternity future, leaving them to perish forever in their sins under His sovereign and just wrath. For the Puritans the wonder of predestination is not that some sinners would be forever lost, for we all deserve that, but that God would save any sinners in His amazing love and grace.

For the Puritans, the doctrine of election is the friend of sinners. If there were no divine election, there would be no hope of salvation. Iain Murray says, "The doctrine of election was vital to the Puritans; they believed with [Jerome] Zanchius that it 'is the golden thread that runs through the whole Christian system,' and they asserted that a departure from this truth would bring the visible church under God's judgment and indignation."[3] Predestination was not mere orthodox theology for the Puritans; it was essential to the gospel and to godliness.[4]

God Sovereignly Creates

Out of His divine abundance and in His sovereign purpose, the Father then commanded creation into being. Thus the cry in Revelation 4:11 goes up to him: "Thou art worthy, O Lord, to receive glory and honour and power: for thou hast created all things, and for thy pleasure they are and were created." And, in keeping with His eternal purpose, creation was brought into being both through and for the Son (Col. 1:15–16). Also in keeping with His character, God created all things good. Sin and evil would be alien infections, not original parts of God's creation.

Because the Puritans took this doctrine of creation seriously, they rejected the sacred-secular dichotomization of life. For them, there was no need to retreat

---

3. Iain Murray, "The Puritans and the Doctrine of Election," in *Puritan Papers, Volume One, 1956–1959*, ed. J. I. Packer (Phillipsburg, N.J.: P & R, 2000), 5. See *The Doctrine of Absolute Predestination* by Girolamo Zanchi (1516–1590), chap. 5.

4. Dewey D. Wallace Jr., *Puritans and Predestination: Grace in English Protestant Theology, 1525–1695* (Chapel Hill: University of North Carolina Press, 1982), 43–44.

to a monastery. As George Swinnock put it, for a Christian should regard "his shop as well as his chapel as holy ground."[5]

God Sovereignly Governs

All this doctrine was thoroughly relevant to the everyday lives of the Puritans, for they went on to affirm that what God has planned and brought into being, He then preserves, sustains, and governs. Nothing falls outside His care and will. Thus He steers His creation, upholding and ruling all things so that they work together to bring about His glorious purposes.

Importantly, God's providential rule over creation extends to all His creatures, all their actions, and whatever befalls them in this life. This truth would prove to be especially consoling and sustaining for the Puritans, given what great suffering they endured. Take John Flavel, author of the Puritan classic *The Mystery of Providence*, as an example. Flavel suffered years of government persecution for his ministry and had to endure the death of his son, as well as the death of three wives in succession. Amid it all, God's providential rule and care was the mainstay of his comfort. This was particularly so since he knew that for the believer, hard providences are no longer marks of divine judgment, but marks of paternal care, flowing from the purpose of the Father for His adopted children. It meant Flavel was able to know profound comfort and hope amid his trials, as he once expressed in this little poem:

> If Satan could see the issue, and th' event
> Of his temptations, he would scarcely tempt.
> Could saints but see what fruits their troubles bring,
> Amidst those troubles they would shout and sing.
> O sacred wisdom! who can but admire
> To see how thou dost save from fire, by fire!
> No doubt but saints in glory wond'ring stand
> At those strange methods few now understand.[6]

---

5. George Swinnock, *The Christian Man's Calling*, in *The Works of George Swinnock*, 5 vols. (Edinburgh: Banner of Truth, 1992), 1:42.

6. John Flavel, *A New Compass for Seamen; or, Navigation Spiritualized*, in *The Works of John Flavel*, 6 vols. (repr., Edinburgh: Banner of Truth, 1968), 5:281.

17

Christ the Mediator

The Puritans at their best were profoundly Christ-centered people. Take "the heavenly Doctor," Richard Sibbes, who wrote in *The Bruised Reed* that "the gracious nature and office of Christ," properly understood, is "the spring of all service to Christ, and comfort from him." Sibbes once preached a sermon on Philippians 1:23–24 entitled "Christ Is Best," in which he compared living faith with dead religion. In dead religion, one can easily talk of receiving "grace" so as to "get heaven." Paul does not. Instead of desiring to depart and be in *heaven*, Paul says he desired to depart and be *with Christ*. For, says Sibbes, "heaven is not heaven without Christ."[1]

The Puritans emphasized that true faith is not about buying into some abstract system of salvation (even one paid for by Christ); first and foremost, it is about Christ by His Word and Spirit bringing me to know, trust, love, and desire Christ Himself. Christ is both the way to know God and to know godliness, so as to become more conformed to His image.

Christ Is the Way to Know God

In a similar vein, John Owen wrote his *Christologia* to argue that true faith is not a mere "notional knowledge" of the Scriptures—it is faith in the person of Christ. Why? Because, he wrote, "faith in Christ is the only means of the true knowledge of God."[2]

This belief meant that the Puritans were outstandingly devotional in their theology. Not that they ever served up "chicken soup for the soul"! Rather, their theology always led to doxology, lifting up the heart in praise to God. Stephen Charnock (1628–1680), who wrote the definitive Puritan work on the attributes of God, his *Discourse on the Existence and Attributes of God*, is a good example. In the midst of another treatise, he could rhapsodize:

1. Sibbes, "Christ Is Best; or, St. Paul's Strait," in *Works*, 1:339.
2. Owen, *Christologia*, in *Works*, 1:77.

Is not God the Father of lights, the supreme truth, the most delectable object?… Is he not light without darkness, love without unkindness, goodness without evil, purity without filth, all excellency to please, without a spot to distaste? Are not all other things infinitely short of him, more below him than a cab of dung is below the glory of the sun?[3]

Whence such gladness in God? Charnock could not have been plainer: true knowledge of the living God is found in and through Christ. But what we see in Christ is so beautiful that it can make the sad sing for joy and the dead spring to life:

Nothing of God looks terrible in Christ to a believer. The sun is risen, shadows are vanished, God walks upon the battlements of love, justice hath left its sting in a Saviour's side, the law is disarmed, weapons out of his hand, his bosom open, his bowels yearn, his heart pants, sweetness and love is in all his carriage. And this is life eternal, to know God believingly in the glories of his mercy and justice in Jesus Christ.[4]

In fact, wrote John Owen, since God only blesses through Christ, it is right for us to say that "the faith of the saints under the Old Testament did principally respect the person of Christ—both what it was, and what it was to be in the fullness of time, when he was to become the seed of the woman."[5]

Christ Is the Way to Godliness

Owen says that the reason we are called to love Christ is because the Father loves Him. His love is the original and origin of love: all the love we see in the world is a copy and shadow of that primary love. Our love for the Son is meant to be a reflection of that first love of the Father's. Thus to be lovingly devoted to the Son is not to dishonor or disregard the Father. Far from it, Owen says: "Therein consists the principal part of our renovation into his image. Nothing renders us so like unto God as our love unto Jesus Christ."[6] Loving the Son, we become like the Father. Also, trusting the Son we become like the Son, for we always become like what we trust. So, when we trust in Christ, we become the kind of person the Father loves. We are conformed to the image of God.

3. Stephen Charnock, *Discourse of the Knowledge of God*, in *The Works of Stephen Charnock*, 5 vols. (repr., Edinburgh: Banner of Truth, 1985), 4:91. "Cab": dialect for "gob" or lump.
4. Charnock, *Discourse of the Knowledge of God*, in *Works*, 4:163.
5. Owen, *Christologia*, in *Works*, 1:101.
6. Owen, *Christologia*, in *Works*, 1:146.

The overall effect of reading Puritan Christology can be summed up simply: it is like reading an invitation. Owen makes that clear:

> Do any of us find decays in grace prevailing in us;—deadness, coldness, lukewarmness, a kind of spiritual stupidity and senselessness coming upon us? Do we find an unreadiness unto the exercise of grace in its proper season, and the vigorous acting of it in duties of communion with God, and would we have our souls recovered from these dangerous diseases? Let us assure ourselves there is no better way for our healing and deliverance, yea, no other way but this alone,—namely, the obtaining a fresh view of the glory of Christ by faith, and a steady abiding therein. Constant contemplation of Christ and his glory, putting forth its transforming power unto the revival of all grace, is the only relief in this case.[7]

For the Puritans, therefore, Christ is supremely precious and altogether lovely. As Thomas Brooks wrote: "Christ is lovely, Christ is very lovely, Christ is most lovely, Christ is always lovely, Christ is altogether lovely.... Christ is the most sparkling diamond in the ring of glory."[8]

---

7. Owen, *The Glory of Christ*, in *Works*, 1:395.
8. Blanchard, comp., *Complete Gathered Gold*, 347.

18

Christ the Compassionate Intercessor

Thomas Goodwin grew up in a God-fearing family in a thoroughly Puritan context. It was unsurprising, then, that from quite a young age his aim in life was to become a preacher. However, he later confessed, his real motivation was that he wanted to become known as one of "the great wits" of the pulpit, for his "masterlust" was the love of applause.

Then in 1620—having just been appointed a fellow of Catharine Hall, Cambridge—he heard a funeral sermon that profoundly moved him, making him deeply concerned for his spiritual state. It was the beginning of seven grim years of introspection as he searched inside himself for signs and marks of grace. Only when he was told to look outwards—to rest on Christ alone—and by grace followed this advice, was he set free. "I am come to this pass now," he said, "that signs will do me no good alone; I have trusted too much to habitual grace for assurance of justification; I tell you Christ is worth all."[1]

Soon afterward he took over for Richard Sibbes, preaching at Holy Trinity Church in Cambridge. It was an appropriate transition, for while in his more introspective days his preaching had been mostly about battering consciences, his appreciation of Christ's free grace now made him a Christ-centered preacher like Sibbes. Sibbes had once told him, "Young man, if ever you would do good, you must preach the gospel and the free grace of God in Christ Jesus"—and that is just what Goodwin now did.

Goodwin's experience served as the context for two of his most popular works, published alongside each other: *Christ Set Forth* and *The Heart of Christ in Heaven towards Sinners on Earth*. He wrote them, he explained, out of his concern that many Christians (like himself once) "have been too much carried away with the rudiments of Christ in their own hearts, and not after Christ himself." Indeed, he warned that "the minds of many are so wholly taken

---

1. "The Memoir of Thomas Goodwin...by His Son," in *The Works of Thomas Goodwin* (repr., Grand Rapids: Reformation Heritage Books, 2006), 2:lxx.

up with their own hearts, that (as the Psalmist says of God) Christ 'is scarce in all their thoughts.'"[2] Goodwin directs us "first to look wholly out of our selves unto Christ," and believed that the reason we don't is, quite simply, because of the "barrenness" of our knowledge of the Lord Jesus Christ.

Thus, Goodwin would model Puritan Christ-centeredness. In *Christ Set Forth*, his goal was to set forth Christ so as to draw our gaze to Him and fill the sails of our faith. In this, he admirably succeeded!

Christ, he explains, is the true object and support of saving faith. And Christ is the cause or ground of all our justification. God has laid up in Christ—through His life, death, resurrection, ascension, and current intercession—everything necessary for our complete justification.

Having ended the first work on Christ's intercession, Goodwin deemed it appropriate then to consider how Christ's heart in heaven is now affected by sinners here on earth. So, Goodwin's companion volume, *The Heart of Christ in Heaven towards Sinners on Earth*, would go on to show from Scripture that in all His heavenly majesty, Christ is not aloof from believers and unconcerned, but has the strongest affections for them. And knowing this, he said, may "hearten and encourage believers to come more boldly unto the throne of grace, unto such a Saviour and High Priest, when they shall know how sweetly and tenderly his heart, though he is now in his glory, is inclined towards them."[3]

Goodwin shows that in all His glorious holiness in heaven, Christ is not distant from His people; if anything, His capacious heart beats more strongly than ever with tender love for them. And in particular, two things stir His compassion: our afflictions and—almost unbelievably—our sins. Indeed, says Goodwin:

> Your very sins move him to pity more than to anger...yea, his pity is increased the more towards you, even as the heart of a father is to a child that hath some loathsome disease.... His hatred shall all fall, and that only upon the sin, to free you of it by its ruin and destruction, but his bowels shall be the more drawn out to you; and this as much when you lie under sin as under any other affliction. Therefore fear not, "What shall separate us from Christ's love?"[4]

How we need Goodwin and his message today! If we are to be delivered from jaded or anxious thoughts of God and a love of sin, we need such a

---

2. Goodwin, *Christ Set Forth*, in *Works*, 4:3.
3. Goodwin, *The Heart of Christ in Heaven towards Sinners on Earth*, in *Works*, 4:95.
4. Goodwin, *The Heart of Christ in Heaven towards Sinners on Earth*, in *Works*, 4:149.

knowledge of Christ. If preachers today could be changed as Goodwin was changed, and preach as Goodwin preached, surely many more believers would then say as he said on his deathbed, "Christ cannot love me better than he doth. I think I cannot love Christ better than I do."[5]

---

5. "Memoir," in Goodwin, *Works*, 2:lxxiv–lxxv.

19

The Holy Spirit

The Holy Spirit was always a special focus in Reformation thought, and particularly by the Puritans. With the exception of the Reformer John Calvin, no theologian before them had undertaken to develop and apply so complete a theology of the Spirit and His work as the Puritans did. Richard Sibbes explained why:

> The more Christ is discovered, the more is the Spirit given; and according to the manifestation of Christ what he hath done for us, and what he hath, the more the riches of Christ is unfolded in the church, the more the Spirit goes along with them. The more the free grace and love of God in Christ alone is made known to the church, the more Spirit there is; and again back again, the more Spirit the more knowledge of Christ.... Now of late for these hundred years, in the time of reformation, there hath been more Spirit and more lightsomeness and comfort. Christians have lived and died more comfortably. Why? *Because Christ hath been more known.*[1]

In the Roman Catholic Church, the work of the Spirit had effectively been replaced by the sacramental system. Among the Quakers, the Spirit was treated in isolation, almost as a different God, delivering experiences and revelations entirely unconnected to Christ and the Scriptures. The Socinians thought of the Spirit as an impersonal force. And in far too many other contexts, the Spirit was simply forgotten or ignored. Against such ideas and tendencies, the Puritans taught that the Spirit is both fully God and fully personal: as God the Holy Ghost, He is one with, but personally distinct from, God the Father and God the Son. In Scripture He is described as having personal qualities: He understands, decides, acts, teaches, and guides; He can be tested, grieved, resisted, quenched, blasphemed, and lied to.

---

1. Sibbes, "The Excellency of the Gospel above the Law," in *Works*, 4:214–15.

The Work of the Spirit

John Owen, in his definitive work on the person and work of the Spirit, *Pneumatologia*, looked at the Spirit's work from creation through to redemption or new creation. The Spirit, he explained, had a quickening, life-giving role in creation. As a dove broods over her eggs, so the Spirit was present in creation, giving life to all living things on earth; and afterwards, He was (and is!) at work in and with the church of God as the plan of redemption unfolded. Throughout the Old Testament, then, the Spirit inspired prophecy and the writing of Scripture, working miracles and enabling people (Samson to be strong, for example, and Bezaleel to be a skillful craftsman). Indeed, "we find everything that is good, even under the Old Testament, assigned unto him [the Spirit] as the sole immediate author of it."[2] The Spirit was then sent down from heaven to light upon and abide with Christ as the incarnate Son of God. Anointed with the Spirit and with power, Christ is made the head of the new creation. For the man Jesus, Owen shows, is the one so anointed with the Spirit that He always acted only as He was equipped and empowered by the Spirit. By the Spirit He was driven into the desert, by the Spirit He Himself then cast out demons, did miracles, offered Himself as a sacrifice, and so on.

From the work of the Spirit in and through Christ, the head of the new creation, Owen proceeds to the work of the Spirit in Christ's body, the church. By the Spirit, the Son gives to us what the Father had given *Him* by the Spirit. Dwelling in Christ as our Head, and in us as the members of His body, the Spirit unites us one to another, to Christ, and to God as our Father in heaven. Whereas we otherwise would merely have cowered before God as our Creator and Judge, now by the Spirit, and with the Son, we cry, "Abba, Father!" Owen concludes: "As the descending of God towards us in love and grace issues or ends in the work of the Spirit in us and on us, so all our ascending towards Him begins therein."[3]

The Spirit and the Christian Life

This belief in the work of the Spirit, for the Puritans, meant that they did not see the Spirit as a mere divine force enabling believers to make some self-improvement. It meant a radically transformative understanding of the Christian life. For the Spirit is the One who has eternally enjoyed and empowered the Word as He goes out from the Father. Through Him the Father has eternally expressed His love for His Son, and through Him the Son has ever loved the Father.

2. Owen, *Pneumatologia*, in *Works*, 3:151.
3. Owen, *Pneumatologia*, in *Works*, 3:200.

In other words, Owen teaches us that when the Father and the Son share the Spirit with us, they share with us *their own life, love, and fellowship*. By the Spirit, we experience the new life of being a child of God in Christ; we begin to share the Father's pleasure in the Son and the Son's in the Father; we begin to love as God loves. Thus Jonathan Edwards wrote that "the divine principle in the saints is of the nature of the Spirit: for as the nature of the Spirit of God is divine love, so divine love is the nature and essence of that holy principle in the hearts of the saints."[4]

From the Father, through the Son, and by the Spirit we as believers are dependent upon the Holy Spirit's saving work in us for every aspect of the order of salvation: our effectual calling, regeneration, repentance, faith, justification, union with Christ, adoption, sanctification, assurance, perseverance, and glorification. Without the Holy Spirit, not a single aspect of our salvation would be realized in our experience; all our Christianity would be a sham, or at best, subscription to a glorious theory. That's why the Puritan Thomas Manton could say, "God's mind is revealed in Scripture, but we can see nothing without the spectacles of the Holy Ghost," and Matthew Henry could write, "All the Holy Spirit's influences are heaven begun, glory in the seed and bud."[5]

---

4. Jonathan Edwards, "Treatise on Grace," in *The Works of Jonathan Edwards*, 26 vols. (New Haven, Conn.: Yale University Press, 1957–2008), 21:191.

5. Blanchard, comp., *Complete Gathered Gold*, 313.

20

Covenant Theology

Since the Puritans strove to base all they taught on the clear teaching of Scripture, it should not surprise us that the scriptural emphasis on covenants would become a prominent feature of their belief system. From near the beginning of the Reformation there had been a growing use among the Reformed of the concept of covenant to organize the Bible's teaching. The Puritans happily and diligently furthered this development. For them, covenant theology includes an exposition of the particular covenants found in the Bible, including the Adamic, Noahic, Abrahamic, Mosaic, and Davidic covenants, culminating in the New Covenant established by Christ (Jer. 31:31; Matt. 26:28).

While Puritans discussed these various covenants, they considered each of them as part of the unfolding of one great covenant, the eternal covenant of grace and reconciliation. That means that they saw the Old Testament covenants as various dispensations or administrations of the one covenant of grace, which was initiated in Genesis 3:15, with God's promise to save Adam and Eve and many of their descendants through a son—"the seed of the woman"—who would conquer Satan. They showed how the key features of this covenant of grace were manifested in all the various biblical covenants. To systematize all of Scripture's teaching, they developed a two-covenant schema, the covenant of works and the covenant of grace; additionally, many argued for a covenant within the covenant of grace, which they called the covenant of redemption.

The Covenant of Works
The Puritans taught that God established a covenant of works with Adam and Eve, promising them life if they obeyed Him and threatening death if they disobeyed by eating of the Tree of Knowledge of Good and Evil. In this covenant of works, which some Puritans also called the covenant of life, Adam represented the entire human race that would descend from him through the ordinary method of procreation. Therefore, when Adam sinned, his guilt was imputed to all his descendants (as their representative head) and his corruption was passed

on to all his descendants (as their natural head). Both he and they were punished, first with spiritual death, becoming dead toward God in trespasses and sins, and in the corruption of their souls, and secondly, with physical death and, in many cases, eternal death. Importantly, they were still bound by the terms of this covenant, and liable to punishment for any further transgressions of it.

The Covenant of Redemption
In eternity, however, the persons of the Godhead had agreed to save Adam and a great number of his descendants in what the Puritans commonly called the covenant of redemption or the "counsel of peace" (Zech. 6:13). By this doctrine they gathered together all that Scripture taught about the plans God laid in eternity to save sinners, including the Father setting His heart on individuals and choosing them for salvation. He gave them to His Son, appointing Him as their Mediator. As the incarnate God-man, the Son would be a "Second Adam," fulfilling the requirements *and* suffering the penalties of the covenant of works—thereby doing all that the first Adam left undone, by way of righteousness, and paying for all that Adam did by his disobedience, by bearing God's wrath.

The covenant of works, then, was fundamental and abiding, being the condition Christ had to fulfill in order to establish the covenant of grace. Following the apostle Paul, the Puritans understood that Christ, as the Second Adam, represented those the Father had given to Him. The Spirit covenanted to apply the benefits that Christ won to all the elect. The terms for entering into the covenant of grace are believing that Jesus is the Messiah, the Son of God, repenting before Him, and trusting Him to save us by His death and resurrection. Saving faith requires the recognition that we are rebels against God and helpless under His wrath and cannot save ourselves from it.

The Covenant of Grace
Faith, not works, is the means by which the Spirit unites us to Christ and brings all of Christ's blessings to us in the covenant of grace. This God-initiated salvation incredibly pardons us of all our sins and covers our continuing weakness through sin—with all its expression in thoughts, words, and deeds, whether sins of commission or omission, whether done deliberately or inadvertently. This plan of God also entails adoption, sanctification, and glorification. Being united to Christ by faith, sinners are called to repent of their sins, strive to put those sins to death, persevere in their faith through every adversity, and live for God's glory (1 Cor. 10:31).

Puritans taught that believers are to rejoice in this covenant of grace because it is the sum of God's promises, sealed with His oath, so that these two things,

God's promise and God's oath, make God's promises doubly certain (Heb. 6:16–18). Because believers' faith is imperfect in this life, they are often beset with sin, and assaulted by doubts and fears that God will not help them. The covenant is a bulwark against such unbelief and an encouragement to faith. The New Testament directs our faith to the sacrifice of Christ on the cross as the only ground of our salvation and the seal of the new and eternal covenant of grace.

Personal and Family Covenanting

The Puritans recommended that individuals make and record their own personal covenants, whereby they confessed what they believed, repented of their particular sins, and committed themselves to follow Christ in new obedience. Such covenants could be quite lengthy and left no room for the modern notion that one can accept Christ only as Savior and not as Lord.

Puritans also affirmed that believers are to rejoice because God's covenant, in its visible manifestation as the church of Christ, includes all who profess faith in Christ, together with their children. As heirs of God's kingdom and of His covenant, the infant children of believers were received into the fellowship of the visible church through baptism, as the sign and seal of the covenant of grace.

The Visible and Invisible Church

The Puritan distinction between the visible and invisible church is usually discussed under the heading of the church. This distinction recognizes that not all members of the visible church are elect or true believers. This distinction applies to the church under the New Covenant, just as it did under the Old. All the members of Abraham's household were circumcised, though all did not believe. Likewise, the Puritans taught that all members of a believer's household are to be baptized, including the children (1 Cor. 7:14), though all might not be or become believers.

Conclusion

Finally, the Puritans also commonly saw God requiring nations and rulers to submit to Christ and His covenant, cherishing the promise that, in the New Covenant age, they would all eventually do so. Therefore, they sought to have the British government enter into covenant with God to maintain and defend the Christian religion in its purity by sustaining the faith, worship, and order of the Reformed church. In these ways, the Puritans utilized the biblical data on covenants to organize the bulk of their teaching with the purpose of showing individuals, churches, and nations their privileges and duties in Christ, the Mediator of the glorious covenant of grace.

PART FOUR

A Saved and Holy People

21

Regeneration

God's effectual calling, which for the Puritans was synonymous with regeneration, meant first of all that a sinner, previously dead in sin, is made alive spiritually. But, like the Reformers, they also on occasion used the word "regeneration" to speak of the believer's whole experience of renewal and transformation, including conversion, faith, repentance, and progressive sanctification or growth in holiness. Normally, however, they distinguished regeneration from the believer's ongoing life of conversion. Stephen Charnock put it this way: "Regeneration is a spiritual change; conversion is a spiritual motion…. Regeneration is a universal change of the whole man; it is as large in renewing as sin was in defacing."[1] In this chapter, we will look only at the first sense of regeneration as the moment of new birth or coming alive spiritually, since like the Puritans, that is the way we most commonly use it today.

For the Puritans this was a subject that required great clarity because of their historic Roman Catholic background, in which regeneration was thought to be the blessed effect of water baptism. Of course, if that were true, then everyone who was baptized—and almost everyone in those days was baptized as an infant—was already regenerated and had no need to be born again. Against this externalistic ritualism, the Puritans labored to show from Scripture that water baptism alone does not make a Christian; as Jesus taught in John 3, we must also be born of the Spirit.

Without the Spirit, the Puritans recognized we are all naturally capable of reforming ourselves *superficially*. The simple desire to get ahead in life, for example, could prompt us to change our behavior, giving up destructive habits for productive ones. What we do not have is the ability to transform ourselves *essentially*: to change our hearts, or to give ourselves new life. This can only be the work of the Holy Spirit, who brings true and radical renewal, taking away our stony hearts of unbelief and making us spiritually alive. For it is the Spirit who is

---

1. Blanchard, comp., *Complete Gathered Gold*, 522.

the Lord and giver of life; it is He who gives life and light, as He did back in the beginning to the dark, lifeless creation.

As Jesus taught, none can enter the kingdom of heaven without being born of the Spirit. Thus, taught John Owen, this work of regeneration had in fact been worked in all the elect under the Old Testament, just as in the New Testament and ever since: "The elect of God were not regenerate one way, by one kind of operation of the Holy Spirit, under the Old Testament, and those under the New Testament [by] another."[2] *Nobody* can, has, or ever will enter the kingdom without being born again of the Spirit.

Given how different this teaching was to what Roman Catholics had grown up with, there was a need to prove that this teaching was both *biblical* and *not a novelty*. Thus Owen, for example, not only brought out scriptural passages on the topic; he also showed how central regeneration was to the thought and experience of the great early church father, Augustine. Owen recounts how the young Augustine was ruled by his appetites and desires, incapable of choosing differently. Then, *using His written Word*, God changed Augustine's heart with all its desires; and with affections now set on Christ, he was able for the first time to choose freely for the good. Without that change in his heart Augustine would have remained a slave to his old ways.

The other confusion in the minds of many was that they erroneously thought that being "born again" had little or nothing to do with hearing the Word of God, and everything to do with extraordinary experiences. The "enthusiasts" as they were known, who promoted such ideas, effectively substituted the Spirit for the Word. The Puritans therefore emphasized that the Spirit *uses means* to affect His work of new birth, and that means is the Word of God. The Word is "the sword of the Spirit" (Eph. 6:17), and it is when Christ is preached through His Word that people are brought out of darkness and into His wonderful light.

Also, the moment of the new birth may not look or seem extraordinary at all; there may be no raptures or ecstasies. In fact, in most cases, there are none. The work of the Spirit, like the motions of the wind, is unseen and can be observed only by its effects. Nor is the Spirit given to destructive violence or tyranny over mankind, as the devil is. In other words, as Owen argued, "He doth not come upon them with involuntary raptures, using their faculties and powers as the evil spirit wrests the bodies of them whom he possesseth."[3] That said, of course, the Spirit will in due course so change believers that the world may come to look

---

2. Owen, *Pneumatologia*, in *Works*, 3:214.
3. Owen, *Pneumatologia*, in *Works*, 3:225.

upon them as quite mad. But that will be because of their lack of conformity to the world and its ways, not their strange experiences, emotional excesses, or eccentric behaviors.

For the Puritans then, just as for Jesus in John 3:3–8, regeneration, which is our second birth, is an absolute necessity. You too, dear reader, must "be born again" (v. 3). Otherwise, as the Puritan William Dyer wrote, "If the second birth hath no place in you, the second death shall have power over you."[4] By "the second death" Dyer means the eternal dying in hell (Rev. 21:8) that those who do not repent and believe in Christ alone for salvation shall experience forever.

---

4. Blanchard, comp., *Complete Gathered Gold*, 522.

22

Faith and Repentance

One who is born again is one who has repented and believed the gospel. That is the nature of our new life in Christ now. However, the Puritans found themselves surrounded by considerable confusion as to what faith and repentance mean.

Misunderstandings of Faith and Repentance
Perhaps the most common error the Puritans had to deal with stemmed from the medieval distinction between "explicit faith" and "implicit faith." Explicit faith, which involved actual knowledge of the truth of the gospel, was considered beyond most people. After all, it was thought, was it even possible for uneducated and feebleminded peasants to grasp the mysteries of the gospel? Thus, it was held that God allowed them to make their way to heaven on the simpler path of "implicit faith," the mere assumption that what the church taught and prescribed was the true way of salvation. Adhering to the church, receiving the sacraments, and doing as her ministers directed, was all one need do to be saved.

For the Puritans, such "implicit faith" fell far short of true and saving faith. In fact, they would argue, the works of such faith amounted to nothing more than self-dependent idolatry because they did not flow from a personal trust in Christ. For faith is not mere visible, physical acts, such as going to church, doing good works, or receiving baptism and the Lord's Supper. Faith will manifest itself in outward acts, yet those acts are simply by-products and signs of faith. Faith itself is a deep, inward matter of the mind and heart and its affections.

Another area of confusion was the idea that saving faith is a simple matter of intellectual assent to the truths of the gospel. But mere agreement is not the same as personal trust. The Puritans gave their classic definition of faith in the Westminster Shorter Catechism (Q. 86), "*What is faith in Jesus Christ? Faith in Jesus Christ is a saving grace, whereby we receive and rest upon him alone for salvation as he is offered to us in the gospel.*" For in faith we do not simply acknowledge the fact that Christ is Lord and Savior: we look to Him, go to Him, receive Him, rest on Him, surrender all to Him, submit to and depend on Him alone as our Lord and Savior (John 3:36; Heb. 12:1–3). Faith involves the heart and the will turning toward truth revealed to the mind. In short, saving faith involves (1) a wholehearted, saving knowledge of God in Christ; (2) a whole-hearted, saving agreement with God's truth about Himself and us and His way of salvation in Christ; and (3) a wholehearted, saving trust in Christ alone as our complete righteousness before God.

Another legacy of the Roman Catholic notion of baptismal regeneration was the idea that faith and repentance can be one-off acts. Thus people would look back at some event in which they had looked to Christ and felt sorrow for sin, and felt that was enough. But, urged the Puritans, true faith does not turn to Christ just once for a mere transaction, to gain heaven. Faith is the continual, trusting, adoring response of the one whose eyes have been opened to see the glory of Christ, to see that he is "the chiefest among ten thousand" (Song 5:10). So, as Richard Sibbes put it: "The true soul that is touched with the Spirit, desires nearer and nearer communion with Christ."[1]

One other important misunderstanding was the idea that faith and repentance are themselves meritorious acts. That is, they are the things we do which earn God's favor and salvation. Now it is true that without faith it is impossible to please God (Heb. 11:6), but that does not mean that faith in itself merits anything. Faith itself is an empty hand, and only brings salvation because it receives and lays hold of Christ, "closing" with Him. Faith is not a creative or meritorious hand, but a receptive hand.

Coming to Christ in Faith and Repentance

In contrast to all these misconceptions, the Puritans held that faith in Christ and repentance from sin are the effects or results of being born again. The Spirit opens our eyes to see both Christ's beauty and our filthiness, and so we abandon our previous self-reliance and self-righteousness, laying hold of Him and resting on Him instead for all our hope and salvation. True faith, in other words, sets its confidence, hope, and desire, not on itself—nor on such things as "grace," "salvation," or "heaven"—but on the Lord of salvation Himself.

Salvation is found in Christ alone, not in faith as such. Faith is not saving because we have faith in our faith; it is saving because its sole object is Christ and His righteousness. The Puritan William Gurnall put it so well: "Faith hath two hands; with one it pulls off its own righteousness and throws it away. With the

---

1. Sibbes, "Bowels Opened," in *Works*, 2:58.

other it puts on Christ's righteousness."[2] It does this by fleeing with all the soul's poverty to Christ's riches, with all the soul's guilt to Christ as reconciler, with all the soul's bondage to Christ as liberator. Thus, the Puritans would advise, though true faith will examine itself, it will be more concerned with looking outward to Him than looking inward at itself.

The necessary, accompanying result of turning to Christ in faith is that we actively turn away from the sin that so offends Him and which is the fruit of unbelief. In this repentance, says the Westminster Confession (15.2),

> a sinner, out of the sight and sense not only of the danger, but also of the filthiness and odiousness of his sins, as contrary to the holy nature, and righteous law of God; and upon the apprehension of His mercy in Christ to such as are penitent, so grieves for, and hates his sins, as to turn from them all unto God, purposing and endeavoring to walk with Him in all the ways of His commandments.

Like the Reformers, then, the Puritans taught that both faith and repentance are daily, lifelong realities for true believers. From the moment of regeneration, Christians are a believing, repenting people. They can't do one without the other. Neither precedes nor follows the other. They are two sides of one coin. Those who repent, believingly repent, looking to Jesus; those who believe, penitently believe, looking to Jesus. Faith and repentance are the sure, essential, ongoing fruits of regeneration. Both are ever looking to Jesus Christ as their sole object.

---

2. Blanchard, comp., *Complete Gathered Gold*, 201.

23

Union with Christ and Justification

For the Puritans, as for the Reformers, there was an important difference—often forgotten today—between *union* with Christ and *communion* with Christ. Communion with Christ—meaning the actual enjoyment of Christ—is something that fluctuates in believers. Sometimes our hearts are full of hallelujahs; sometimes they are frosty and unfeeling toward Christ. That wavering warmth of communion, however, was not seen by the Puritans as the foundation of our union with Christ. Quite the opposite. Believers are born again into a union with Christ which is guaranteed and stable, the solid foundation on which we can enjoy communion with Him. As Richard Sibbes put it: "Union is the foundation of communion."[1]

The Bridegroom and His Bride
The biblical image Sibbes and others turned to most frequently to illustrate union with Christ is that of Christ as the loving royal Bridegroom and the church as His bride. The contrast with the Roman Catholic teaching that people in the sixteenth century had been brought up with was striking. That teaching portrayed Christ as a distant figure, doling out His grace from afar, approachable only through other mediators such as priests and saints. Before Him one could never have confidence or experience intimacy. But if Christ is the church's loving Bridegroom, what place is there for mediators between Him and us? And what now would the church want from Him? Not some *thing* called "grace," but the Bridegroom Himself, freely and wholly offered.

The Joyful Exchange
Sibbes unpacked this image in a sermon series he preached on the Song of Solomon, showing how Christ, our great Bridegroom, has joined Himself to His bride; taken on Himself our sin, death, and judgment; and imparted to us His life

---

1. Sibbes, "Bowels Opened," in *Works*, 2:174.

and perfect righteousness. He has become poor that we might receive His riches. In other words, because of our union with Christ, believers are justified and declared righteous in God's sight with the very righteousness of Christ. Good works will flow as a *result* not a *cause* of the Christian's righteousness. As the bride shares the status of her Bridegroom, so Christians share—or rather, have imputed to them—the righteous status of Christ. It is what Luther called the "joyful exchange." Christ is one with His people, and so all theirs is His, and all His is theirs. Thus, said Sibbes, Christians are able to confess:

> Often think with thyself, What am I? a poor sinful creature; but I have a righteousness in Christ that answers all. I am weak in myself, but Christ is strong, and I am strong in him. I am foolish in myself, but I am wise in him. What I want [lack] in myself I have in him. He is mine, and his righteousness is mine, which is the righteousness of God-man. Being clothed with this, I stand safe against conscience, hell, wrath, and whatsoever. Though I have daily experience of my sins, yet there is more righteousness in Christ, who is mine, and who is the chief of ten thousand, than there is sin in me.[2]

With this belief in a justifying righteousness found only in Christ, the Puritans were able to show believers that our confidence can and should rest, not on our strength of faith or performance, but upon Christ. For it is in the Son's merits, and not our own, that Christians are righteous.

Differences over Justification

Though Puritans tended to agree on most truths, there wasn't complete agreement on the doctrine of justification among all the Puritans. Richard Baxter (1615–1691) taught that Christians need a *double* righteousness for their salvation: Christ's righteousness fulfills the demands of the old covenant for us, but, Baxter argued, believers still need to be justified on the basis of the "new law" of the gospel. In effect, my faith becomes the basis of my righteousness.

The vast majority of the Puritans, including men like John Owen and Robert Traill, argued that such reasoning was fundamentally wrongheaded and unscriptural. Scripture does not direct us to our own faith as the bedrock of our confidence, but to Christ. In Romans 5:12–21 we see especially clearly that it is because of the righteousness of Christ alone that we are counted righteous. He and He alone is our righteousness. So, wrote Traill:

---

2. Sibbes, "Bowels Opened," in *Works*, 2:147.

If a man trusts to his own righteousness, he rejects Christ's; if he trusts to Christ's righteousness, he rejects his own. If he will not reject his own righteousness, as too good to be renounced, if he will not venture on Christ's righteousness, as not sufficient alone to bear him out, and bring him safe off at God's bar, he is in both a convicted unbeliever. And if he endeavour to patch up a righteousness before God, made up of both, he is still under the law, and a despiser of gospel-grace (Gal. 2:21).[3]

In Westminster's Shorter Catechism, therefore, the Puritans defined justification as "an act of God's free grace, wherein He pardoneth all our sins, and accepteth us as righteous in His sight, only for the righteousness of Christ imputed to us, and received by faith alone" (Q. 33). The Puritans relished the fact that Christ's righteousness exceeds our sinfulness. Do you, like them, find comfort, security, and eternal life in this grand, amazing gospel truth?

---

3. Robert Traill, *Justification Vindicated*, Puritan Paperbacks (Edinburgh: Banner of Truth, 2002), 70.

24

Adoption

Another striking difference between medieval Roman Catholic and Reformation theology was the emphasis the Reformers—and later the Puritans—put
upon the fact that in salvation God adopts those whom He saves as His children
and heirs.

Calvin on Adoption

In his *Institutes*, John Calvin wrote that our very problem as sinners is that in
"this ruin of mankind *no one now experiences God either as Father* or as Author
of salvation, or favorable in any way, until Christ the Mediator comes forward
to reconcile him to us."[1] The Son's task in redemption, then, was precisely "so to
restore us to God's grace as to make of the children of men, children of God; of
the heirs of Gehennna, heirs of the Heavenly Kingdom."[2] And indeed the first title
of the Spirit given in Scripture is:

> the "Spirit of adoption" because he is the witness to us of the free bene-
> volence of God with which God the Father has embraced us in his beloved
> only-begotten son to become a Father to us; and he encourages us to have
> trust in prayer. In fact, he supplies the very words so that we may fearlessly
> cry, "Abba, Father!" [Rom. 8:15; Gal. 4:6].[3]

The Puritans on Adoption

This was the theology that would be championed, developed, and applied by the
Puritans.[4] They wanted believers to see that union with Christ not only means

---

1. John Calvin, *Institutes of the Christian Religion*, trans. Ford Lewis Battles, ed. John T.
McNeill, Library of Christian Classics (Philadelphia: Westminster, 1960), 1.2.1, our emphasis.
2. Calvin, *Institutes*, 2.12.2.
3. Calvin, *Institutes*, 3.1.3.
4. See Joel R. Beeke, *Heirs with Christ: The Puritans on Adoption* (Grand Rapids: Reformation
Heritage Books, 2008).

that Christians are clothed with the *righteous* status of the Son; they also get to share His status of *beloved* Son before the Father. In other words, Christians are not only accounted righteous before the heavenly Judge; we are embraced as children by a heavenly Father.

It is not that believers become *more* adopted the more we are transformed in Christlikeness. Our adoption—like our righteousness—is sealed in Christ the moment we are born again and united to Christ. United to Christ we can know we share the very standing of our firstborn Brother before God our Father. Indeed, taught the Puritans, the comfort this affords to believers is precisely a motivation to love our Father and to grow in His likeness. Richard Sibbes once showed beautifully how this truth of our adoption flows from our union with Christ. God the Father, he said,

> can as soon cease to love his Son, as cease to love us. For with the same love he loveth all Christ mystical, head and members. There is not the least finger of Christ, the least despised member of Christ, but God looketh on him with that sweet eternal tenderness with which he looketh upon his Son, preserving the prerogative of the head. Oh, this is a sweet comfort, that now all the excellent privileges of a Christian are set on Christ and then on us and therefore we should not lose them, for Christ will lose nothing.[5]

This, the Puritans knew, was profoundly comfort-giving, worship-inspiring theology—that out of pure grace we sinners are compelled to cry, "Behold, what manner of love the Father hath bestowed upon us, that we should be called the sons of God" (1 John 3:1). It is life-transforming theology, and just the truth we need for a healthy, reverent, and enjoyable prayer life.

The Westminster Confession of Faith (chap. 12) sums up the privileges the Puritans saw Christians have through our adoption in Christ:

> All those that are justified, God vouchsafeth, in and for His only Son Jesus Christ, to make partakers of the grace of adoption, by which they are taken into the number, and enjoy the liberties and privileges of the children of God, have His name put upon them, receive the spirit of adoption, have access to the throne of grace with boldness, are enabled to cry, Abba, Father, are pitied, protected, provided for, and chastened by Him as by a Father: yet never cast off, but sealed to the day of redemption; and inherit the promises, as heirs of everlasting salvation.

5. Sibbes, "A Heavenly Conference," in *Works*, 6:460–61.

Transformed Relationships Flowing Out of Adoption

In his exposition of 1 John 3, the New England Puritan John Cotton shows believers that a conscious sense of our spiritual adoption in Christ transforms all our relationships in this life. First, it transforms our relationship *to God* (1 John 3:1a), for it makes us want to do the will of our Father and gives us security in belonging to His heavenly household as his *bona fide* sons in Christ, despite our remaining indwelling sin. Cotton writes, "We are the sons of God even now, though there is much unbelief in our hearts, and much weakness and many corruptions within us."[6]

Second, adoption also changes our relationship *to the world* (1 John 3:1b). Just as the believer shares with Jesus the ineffable love of the Father, he likewise shares with Jesus the hostility, estrangement, and hatred of the world. "If God saw it meet [fitting] that his Son should be afflicted in the world," Cotton writes, "let us not think we shall go to heaven…without also drinking of the same cup that he drank of."[7]

Third, adoption transforms our relationship *to the future* (1 John 3:2). Cotton stresses that God is changing us now because we are His sons, but when Christ will appear on the clouds, we will fully bear the image of our elder brother Jesus without spot or wrinkle. What a future! As sons of God, we ought to live in anticipation of it.

Fourth, adoption transforms our relationship *to ourselves* (1 John 3:3: "Every man that hath this hope in him purifieth himself, even as he is pure"). That is, the adopted seek to purify themselves daily, using Christ as their pattern. Consequently, Cotton says, "Every child of God has hope in Christ, to be made like him at his appearing."[8]

Finally, adoption transforms our relation *to the church* as the family of God (1 John 3:14–18). Once we belong to this large family as sons of God, says Cotton, "the sons of God ought to be the men of our love and delight."[9] Then we are made willing even to lay down our life for our brother or sister (v. 16).

Adoption therefore transforms our entire lives.

---

6. John Cotton, *An Exposition of First John* (Evansville, Ind.: Sovereign Grace, 1962), 319.
7. Cotton, *An Exposition of First John*, 318.
8. Cotton, *An Exposition of First John*, 327–29.
9. Cotton, *An Exposition of First John*, 316.

Conclusion: The Crowning Privileges of Adoption

Our crowning privilege of adoption, said the Puritans, is *heirship*. God's adopted children are all royal heirs apparent and coheirs with Christ (Rom. 8:16–17). In that heirship, all the benefits of the covenant of grace—God's entire heavenly treasure including Himself as God and Father—accrue to His adopted children.

Because you are adopted, dear believer, your heavenly Father engrafts you into His family, moves you to rejoice in intimate communion with Him and His Son, gives you freedom to know Him and call upon Him as your Father, gifts you with the Spirit of adoption, and strengthens your faith through His fatherly promises and prayer. As your Father, He corrects and chastens you for your sanctification, comforts you with His love and pity, counsels and directs you, provides you with Christian liberty, preserves you and keeps you from falling, and provides you with every covenant mercy that you need in this life and for a better life to come.

Let us, like Jeremiah Burroughs, revel in this glorious truth of adoption: "Oh, who can utter the soul-satisfying, soul-ravishing consolation there is in this, that the same God that is the God of Jesus Christ is my God, and the same Father that is the Father of Jesus Christ is my Father!"[10]

---

10. Jeremiah Burroughs, *The Saint's Happiness, or Lectures on the Beatitudes* (1867; repr., Beaver Falls, Pa.: Soli Deo Gloria Publications, 1988), 193.

25

Sanctification

From the earliest days of the Reformation, the basic Roman Catholic objection to the Reformed doctrine of justification by faith alone is that it makes men "careless and profane" (Heidelberg Catechism, Q. 64). That is, believing this doctrine church members will cease to pursue holiness of life in the fear of God. But like the Reformers, the Puritans insisted that, "It is impossible that those, who are implanted into Christ by a true faith, should not bring forth the fruits of thankfulness," or the "things that accompany salvation" (Heb. 6:9). They strongly insisted that holiness is not a prerequisite of justification but rather a necessary consequence, result, or fruit of it—and they were passionate about that vital distinction. John Owen wrote, "It is the eternal and immutable purpose of God, that all who are his in a peculiar manner, all whom he designs to bring unto blessedness in the everlasting enjoyment of himself, shall antecedently thereunto be made holy."[1]

After his initial, instantaneous work of regeneration, the Spirit always works progressively to sanctify those who are His new creation. Hence the classic Puritan definition of sanctification in the Westminster Shorter Catechism (Q. 35): "Sanctification is the work of God's free grace, whereby we are renewed in the whole man after the image of God, and are enabled more and more to die unto sin, and live unto righteousness."

The Idea of Sanctification
This Puritan idea of sanctification includes three elements: First, sanctification is rooted in the character or essence of God. You can't understand holiness without understanding God's holiness, which shows the separateness of God from all His creation and from all that is evil. Since God is holy, He cannot be approached by sinners apart from an infinite and holy sacrifice, which only His Son can give (Lev. 17:11; Heb. 9:22).

---

1. Owen, *Pneumatologia*, in *Works*, 3:591.

Second, sanctification is God's gracious work that involves both our state and our condition before Him. Our state as believers is one of holiness in Christ from the moment we are born again. In that same moment that we are born again, we are justified by God, and enter into a state of holiness before Him. That is our position, but our practice of holiness has a long way to go. The Puritans compared this to marriage. When a couple gets married they enter the state of oneness, but their actually becoming one takes a lifetime of marriage, and even then is not fully realized. So when a Christian is born again and justified by faith, He becomes one with Christ in His state before God, but to always be one with Christ in his daily condition is something else. The Spirit progressively directs and aids the believer in becoming one with Christ in his practice; this work of sanctification is never complete in this life. While positionally holy, and wholly free from the penalty of sin, we must daily engage with sin—especially indwelling sin—in holy warfare as long as we dwell in earthly bodies and until our last breath.

Third, sanctification is comprehensive ("the whole man," Q. 35 says), and expresses itself in ongoing repentance and in righteousness (increasingly dying to sin and living to righteousness, Q. 35 says). The repentance dimension in sanctification guarantees that the believer's life continues to remain a changed life because, as the Puritans taught, repentance involves much more than saying, "I'm sorry"; it involves a changed life, resulting from the conviction and hatred of sin (Ps. 51:1–4), and the confessing and forsaking of sin (Prov. 28:13). Thus, the whole life of the believer is impacted by sanctification. Every part of us is called to walk in Christ's holiness.

An "Inside Out" Work
The Puritans didn't just place sanctification after (rather than before) justification: their very understanding of holiness was quite different from that of Roman Catholics. In Roman Catholicism, the root of our problem before God tends to be located in our behavior: we have done wrong things and we need to start doing right things. The Puritans plumbed much deeper. They knew that the outward acts of sin are merely the manifestations of the desires of the heart (James 1:14–15; Eph. 2:3). Merely to alter a person's behavior without changing those desires cultivates hypocrisy, the self-righteous cloak for a cold and vicious heart. And, they would note, religious systems that merely sought to alter behavior were invariably cruel, based on what we call guilt-tripping or browbeating. No, hearts must be turned, and evil desires eclipsed by stronger ones for Christ.

As pastors, the Puritans therefore saw themselves as spiritual heart doctors. They wanted their people to love the Lord with all their hearts; they wanted them to truly hate their sin, and not merely dread the thought of God's punishment of it. In other words, they saw that true holiness and growth in Christlikeness happens *inside out*: it starts deep inside the affections and desires of the heart and then manifests itself in outward godly behavior.

Realizing the Gospel in Our Souls

How then does the Spirit effect this deep change in our hearts? Primarily, through exciting and affecting us by the gospel, making us acquire a taste for the Lord and His ways. In fact, wrote John Owen, "holiness is nothing but the implanting, writing, and realizing of the gospel in our souls."[2] And that being the case, it must happen in the same way as our initial salvation. That is, just as we are justified by the blood of Christ, so we are sanctified by the blood of Christ. "The Holy Ghost," said Owen, "actually communicates the cleansing, purifying virtue of the blood of Christ unto our souls and consciences, whereby we are freed from shame, and have boldness towards God."[3] By faith, then, our consciences are freed from guilt and we are able to grow in heartfelt love for God, which is the essence of holiness.

Richard Sibbes put it like this:

> Tenderness of heart is wrought by an apprehension of tenderness and love in Christ. A soft heart is made soft by the blood of Christ.... As when things are cold, we bring them to the fire to heat and melt, *so we bring our cold hearts to the fire of the love of Christ*.... If you will have this tender and melting heart, then *use the means of grace;* be always under the sunshine of the gospel.[4]

That is, by revealing Christ to me, the Spirit turns my heart from its natural hatred of God toward a sincere love for Him. Therefore, just as the free grace of God in Christ Jesus is the means by which the hearts of sinners are first turned to God, it is likewise the primary means by which the hearts of believers continue to be turned from the love for sin to love for God.

---

2. Owen, *Pneumatologia*, in *Works*, 3:370–71.
3. Owen, *Pneumatologia*, in *Works*, 3:445.
4. Sibbes, "The Tender Heart," in *Works*, 6:33, 41.

Keeping in Step with the Spirit

The fact that sanctification is the Spirit's work in us does not mean that Christians passively "let go and let God." Those who are given life by the Spirit will begin to hate sin and actively want to put it to death (which theologians call *mortification*). Just so, with their hearts turned to love for Christ, they will want to know Him better, be like Him, and walk in His ways (which theologians call *vivification*, or "the quickening of the new man"). And the more they grow in godliness, the more vigorously they will fight sin and chase righteousness.

When the believer is walking in step with the Spirit, he will pursue trinitarian godliness, seeking the Spirit's grace to imitate the character of the Father (Lev. 11:44), to conform to the image of Christ (Phil. 2:5–8), and to submit to the mind of the Holy Spirit as revealed in Scripture (Rom. 8:6). That pursuit will involve diligently using the means—spiritual disciplines—God has provided to grow holiness in His people. The Puritans spoke of these disciplines in three categories: *private disciplines* (read and search the Scriptures, meditate on the Scriptures, pray, listen to sermons, read God-glorifying literature, and spiritual journaling), *family disciplines* (family worship, spiritual conversation, and hospitality), and *corporate disciplines* (the preached Word, the sacraments, communion of the saints, and sanctifying of the entire Lord's Day). For growth in sanctification, the believer is dependent on the Spirit of God as he diligently engages in the spiritual disciplines. It is the Spirit's work to make these means effectual to us as we persevere in using them.

Conclusion: Beautiful for Eternity

Holiness, taught Jonathan Edwards, is not a sour, sad thing: it is the unspotted beauty of God Himself. The Spirit's work of sanctification, then, is to heal believers of the sin that scars, to make them whole, and to grow them in divine beauty. It is the beginning of the new creation being realized, a work that will be perfected in our resurrection.

26

Assurance of Salvation

The Puritans wrote much on assurance of grace and salvation. They defined this assurance as the conviction that one belongs to Christ through faith and will enjoy everlasting salvation. A person who has assurance not only believes in Christ's righteousness as his salvation but knows for certain that he believes, and that he is graciously chosen, loved, and forgiven by the Father for the sake of Christ, who has died for him and continues to pray for him in heaven. Personal assurance is found in its fruits such as close fellowship with God, childlike trust, willing obedience, thirsting after God, unspeakable joy and peace in the triune God for Christ's sake, and longing to glorify Him by carrying out the Great Commission.

William Perkins on Assurance

One of the greatest Puritan writers on assurance was William Perkins. Perkins's writing on assurance of faith set the agenda for the seventeenth century and for chapter 18 of the Westminster Confession of Faith. He wrote several books in the late 1580s and 1590s that explain how one may know he is saved: *A Golden Chaine: Or, The Description of Theologie: Containing the Order of the Causes of Salvation and Damnation;*[1] *A Treatise Tending unto a Declaration, Whether a Man Be in the Estate of Damnation or in the Estate of Grace; A Case of Conscience, the Greatest That Ever Was: How a Man May Know Whether He Be the Childe of God or No; A Discourse of Conscience: Where Is Set Down the Nature, Properties, and Differences Thereof: As Also the Way to Get and Keepe a Good Conscience;* and *A Graine of Musterd-Seede: Or, the Least Measure of Grace That Is or Can Be Effectuall to Salvation.*[2]

---

1. William Perkins, *A Golden Chain,* in *The Works of William Perkins,* ed. Joel R. Beeke and Derek W. H. Thomas, 10 vols. (Grand Rapids: Reformation Heritage Books, 2015–2020), 6:1–272.
2. All four of these treatises may be found in Perkins, *Works,* vol. 8.

Through his prolific writings, Perkins taught people how to search their consciences for even the least evidence of election based on Christ's saving work. Perkins viewed such efforts as part of the pastor's fundamental task to keep "balance in the sanctuary" between divine sovereignty and human responsibility.[3] Sinners had to be shown how God's immovable will moved the will of man and how to look for evidences of election and inclusion in God's covenant. They also had to be taught how to make their election sure by living in this world as the elect of God.

Grounds of Assurance

Perkins proposed three grounds of assurance: (1) the promises of the gospel, which are contained in God's covenant and are confirmed or ratified by the shedding of Christ's blood as the blood of the covenant; (2) the testimony of the Holy Spirit witnessing with our spirit that we are the children of God; and (3) the fruits of sanctification. These three interconnected grounds, all of which depend on the illuminating and applying ministry of the Holy Spirit, are so important that Perkins called them "the hinge upon which the gate of heaven turns."[4] The believer ought always to strive to grow in assurance by seeking as large a degree of assurance as possible from all three of these grounds or categories of evidence.

The promises of God are always the primary ground of assurance. When embraced by faith, the promises of God produce the fruits of sanctification and are confirmed in our hearts by the witness or testimony of the Spirit. The believer may have difficulty at times realizing one or more of these grounds in his own experience. That is particularly true of the testimony of the Spirit, in which the Spirit witnesses powerfully with the believer's spirit through the Word of God that Christ is his and he is Christ's. Yet that ought not to distress the believer, Perkins says, because even when the Spirit's testimony is not felt deeply enough to persuade the believer of his election, the effects of the Spirit's work will be demonstrated in sanctification.

In his writings, Perkins lists various marks or works of sanctification that the believer, in dependency on the Spirit, can use to grow his assurance. Here is one such list:

(1) To feel our wants, and in the bitterness of heart to bewail the offense of God in every sin. (2) To strive against the flesh—that is, to resist, and to hate the ungodly motions thereof and with grief to think them burdensome and

---

3. Irvonwy Morgan, *Puritan Spirituality* (London: Epworth Press, 1973), ch. 2.
4. Perkins, *Commentary on Galatians*, in *Works*, 2:260.

troublesome. (3) To desire earnestly and vehemently the grace of God and merit of Christ to obtain eternal life. (4) When it is obtained, to account it a most precious jewel (Phil. 3:8). (5) To love the minister of God's Word, in that he is a minister; and a Christian, in that he is a Christian—and for that cause, if need require, to be ready to spill our blood with them (Matt. 10:42; 1 John 3:16). (6) To call upon God earnestly, and with tears. (7) To desire and love Christ's coming and the day of judgment, that an end may be made of the days of sin. (8) To flee all occasions of sin and seriously to endeavor to come to newness of life. (9) To persevere in these things to the last gasp of life.[5]

Perkins taught that if a believer has, even to a small degree, experienced some of these marks of grace, he can be assured that he is being sanctified by the Spirit of God. All of these marks are alien or "unnatural" to those who are dead in trespasses and sins. In turn, since the entire golden chain of salvation— election, vocation (effectual calling), faith, justification, sanctification, and eternal glorification—are "inseparable companions," the believer "may infallibly conclude in his own heart that he has and shall have interest in all the others in his due time."[6]

Trinitarian Framework
Perkins was keenly aware of the need to set all marks of grace in a trinitarian framework so that they did not result in a man-centered religion. In commenting on 1 John 4:7, Perkins wrote that believers know God "by a special knowledge, whereby they are assured that God, the Father of Christ, is their Father; Christ, their Redeemer; the Holy Spirit, their Sanctifier."[7] All assurance is Christological. It is based on Christ's merits (commenting on 1 John 2:12), received by faith in Him (on 1 John 5:4), and patterned after Him in sanctification (on 1 John 3:3).[8] It depends on Christ's anointing with the Spirit, in which all believers share. Perkins viewed the "unction" or "anointing" John refers to in 1 John 2:20, 27 as the grace of God's Holy Spirit that we receive from Christ, which is the fulfilment of the anointings with holy oil in the Old Testament.[9]

In sum, the believer may be assured of his adoption by God the Father by discerning the marks of saving grace in his heart and life as they flow out of Christ

---

5. Perkins, *A Golden Chain*, in *Works*, 6:262–63.
6. Perkins, *The Whole Treatise of the Cases of Conscience*, in *Works*, 8:153.
7. Perkins, *A Case of Conscience*, in *Works*, 8:609.
8. Perkins, *A Case of Conscience*, in *Works*, 8:602, 611, 605.
9. Perkins, *A Case of Conscience*, in *Works*, 8:603–4.

and are produced in him by the Holy Spirit, who witnesses with the believer's conscience that the believer is a child of God.

Concluding Application

From Perkins, we need to learn that it is still critical today that you strive to make your calling and election sure. Strive to get as much assurance as you can, with the Spirit's enlightening grace, from the promises of God, the testimony of the Holy Spirit, and the marks of saving, sanctifying grace.

27

Perseverance

The possibility of peace with God and assurance in the face of death were at the heart of Martin Luther's struggles which precipitated the Reformation. And similar questions persisted into Puritan times—especially, can a true believer fall out of union with Christ and finally be damned? The Puritans knew the pastoral importance of this question and answered it repeatedly and emphatically: *no!*

True Saints Will Persevere
John Owen summarized some of the main reasons for this Puritan belief and why the Puritans defended it so emphatically in his *Doctrine of the Saints' Perseverance Explained and Confirmed* (1654). In it, he wrote:

> That you and all the saints of God may yet enjoy that peace and consolation which is in believing that the eternal love of God is immutable, that he is faithful in his promises, that his covenant, ratified in the death of his Son, is unchangeable, that the fruits of the purchase of Christ shall be certainly bestowed on all them for whom he died, and that everyone who is really interested in these things shall be kept unto salvation, is the aim of my present plea and contest.[1]

In other words, Owen held to a robustly trinitarian belief that God will finish in us what He has started in us (Phil. 1:3–6; 1 Peter 1:3–5).

First, the Father has purposed and promised the final salvation of His people. He is not fickle in nature, but immutable, unchanging, and unchangeable. Therefore, His purposes and promises are fixed and immutable. They are not dependent on our circumstances. Rather, His purposes *determine* all our circumstances. Thus when, for example, we read that none shall snatch believers out of His hand (John 10:27–29), we may trust these promises of God.

---

1. Owen, *The Doctrine of the Saints' Perseverance Explained and Confirmed*, in *Works*, 11:5–6.

Second, the covenant has been fulfilled by Jesus Christ. As the sacrifice for our sin, He has atoned for all the sins of all His people and satisfied the demands of divine justice and the law. As our great high priest, and on the basis of His own sacrifice, He now effectively intercedes at the right hand of God. Having bought His people at the cost of His own blood, He would never suffer the loss of what He had lived and died for—to save all those whom the Father had given Him.

Third, the Spirit has been sent specifically to unite believers to Christ, to dwell in them, and to conform them to the image of Christ. The Spirit is therefore the earnest of our inheritance (Eph. 1:14). But what sort of earnest would He be if those whom He has sealed could finally fall away? And if He truly does unite believers to Christ, then the falling away of a believer would be the unthinkable chopping off of a member from the body of Christ.

Three brief notes of clarification should be made here. First, through Scripture and the history of the church we do see individuals who apostatize or fall away from their profession of faith in Christ. However, that does not prove that saints can fall out of salvation; only that those apostates were never true believers. Second, the Puritans taught that true saints can temporarily appear to have fallen away. Believers stumble. They may *fall into sin*, but they will not indefinitely *live in sin*. Owen pointed out this difference when he said that the difference between an unbeliever and a believer is that an unbeliever clings to sin willingly while sin clings to the believer against his will. Third, and similarly, they did not take this to mean that believers are never troubled by any lack of assurance. While God knows and keeps those who are His, from our perspective persevering is hard work. We fight against sin and labor to grow in holiness and stay faithful. Persevering is not the same as coasting.

Objections to the Doctrine of Perseverance
This doctrine was not and has never been without its detractors. It is, they claim, (1) unbiblical, (2) unpractical, and (3) unholy.

> (1) It is unbiblical, they argue, because of "falling away" passages such as Hebrews 6:1–8 and 10:26–39. The Puritans counter by noting that the New Testament letters were written to and concerned whole congregations, and there are always tares amid the wheat of God's harvest-field. That is why such warnings are necessary. Thus we can read of Hymenaeus and Philetus "erring" or wandering away from the truth (2 Tim. 2:17–18), and then go straight on to read in the next verse: "Nevertheless the foundation of God standeth sure, having this seal, The Lord knoweth them that are his" (v. 19).

(2) It is unpractical, it is alleged, because who has the ability to be faithful to the end? The Puritans answer this by asserting that we are kept not by our own ability but by God's power (1 Peter 1:5).

(3) It is unholy, opponents state, because it removes the motivation from believers to live holy lives. That is another misunderstanding the Puritans address. The Spirit who comes to unite us to Christ also comes to conform us to His image. He is the Spirit of holiness who enables believers to grow in faithfulness and holiness, and thus to persevere. Moreover, this doctrine is paramount for promoting true love for God. Thomas Watson put it like this: "A Christian's main comfort depends upon this doctrine of perseverance. Take this away, and you prejudice religion, and cut the sinews of all cheerful endeavors."[2] For without this doctrine we would be discouraged and unable to approach God with gospel liberty and love. And without that love, there would be no true obedience. God's loving and comforting promises do not promote but destroy the power of sin in us.

---

2. Thomas Watson, *A Body of Practical Divinity,* in *The Select Works of the Rev. Thomas Watson* (New York: Robert Carter & Brothers, 1855), 186.

28

Heaven, a World of Love

The Puritans tended to be a heavenly-minded people, a people who thought of themselves—like Bunyan's hero from *Pilgrim's Progress*—as travelers on pilgrimage to the Celestial City. They thought and wrote a good deal on the rest and glory promised to God's children, and so we could turn to many of them for extensive treatment of the last things. But at the end of this book it seems appropriate to bring in Jonathan Edwards (1703–1758), a Puritan born out of time (in the eighteenth century) and place (in New England), after Puritanism as a movement had almost disappeared from England.

In 1738, in Northampton, Massachusetts, Edwards preached a series of sermons on 1 Corinthians 13, the last of which was entitled "Heaven Is a World of Love." In the sermon he describes heaven as the garden, palace, temple, and presence-chamber of God. He concludes:

> And this renders heaven a world of love; for God is the fountain of love, as the sun is the fountain of light. And therefore the glorious presence of God in heaven fills heaven with love, as the sun placed in the midst of the hemisphere in a clear day fills the world with light.[1]

The image is taken especially from Revelation 21 and 22, where the glory of God and of the Lamb fills the New Jerusalem with light, expelling all darkness. This light of God's love and glory makes all who are there both holy and happy. Thus everyone there becomes altogether lovely; not a spot of evil or sin or pollution infects heaven.

There the church will be presented to Christ as a bride clothed in fine linen, clean and white, without spot or wrinkle (Eph. 5:25–27). Bridegroom and bride will delight in each other as the love of God flows from God to Christ the Head of the church, and through Him to all who are His. As the love of God radiates in responding love, all of heaven's inhabitants will rejoice in Him, saints

1. Edwards, "Charity and Its Fruits," in *Works*, 8:369.

and angels together. Suffused with that divine love, angels and saints will also then perfectly love one another. In other words, Edwards says, we will be like flowers in the garden of God, unfurling and blossoming in the sunshine of God's love and giving off a heavenly fragrance:

> All shall stand about the God of glory, the fountain of love, as it were opening their bosoms to be filled with those effusions of love which are poured forth from thence, as the flowers on the earth in a pleasant spring day open their bosoms to the sun to be filled with his warmth and light, and to flourish in beauty and fragrancy by his rays. Every saint is as a flower in the garden of God, and holy love is the fragrancy and sweet odor which they all send forth, and with which they fill that paradise.[2]

What Edwards is envisaging here is the full blooming of that heavenly seed of love for God which was first implanted in Christians at their regeneration. That tiny seed makes believers long now for holiness and the presence of the Lord. But in that day all that heavenly desire will be consummated, and that love for God will be perfected.

In typical Puritan fashion, Edwards then applies this vision of heaven to his hearers. Turning to unbelievers, he entreats them to consider all they will miss. For in terrible contrast, they face hell, a world of hate where there is no love and everything is hateful—the terrible sink and pit of God's judgment. As for believers, he calls them earnestly to seek heaven, to fill their eyes with that hope and so grow tired of this fallen world. Instead of indulging in the pursuit of earthly things, Edwards urges believers to fix their thoughts constantly on heaven:

> You cannot earnestly and constantly seek heaven without having your thoughts much there. Therefore turn the current of your thoughts and meditations towards that world of love, and that God of love who dwells there, and towards Christ who is ascended and sits there at the right hand of God; and towards the blessed enjoyments of that world. And be much in conversing with [God and Christ,] without which heaven is no heaven.[3]

Dear believer, as heaven our home is a world of love, so in anticipation we should live now a life of love. That is the way to live for those who have that heavenly seed of love in them.

---

2. Edwards, "Charity and Its Fruits," in *Works*, 8:386.
3. Edwards, "Charity and Its Fruits," in *Works*, 8:395.

PART FIVE

Christ's Bride

29

Church and Worship

The Reformation brought a revolution in worship. In the Middle Ages, the church focused its worship on an altar and an image of Christ dying on the cross. The priest performed complicated rituals to offer sacrifices to God while chanting in Latin—a language only educated people understood. In many ways, the Puritans were just carrying out the changes in worship begun by Martin Luther and developed by John Calvin. The Reformers abolished worship of man-made images, sacred objects, and holy rituals and restored the focus of worship to the simple adoration of God through Christ as regulated by His own commandments.

The Knowledge of God in Worship

The most basic principle of Puritan worship was to know the true God. William Perkins said, "When God is not known aright, He is not worshipped aright, but either the idols of our brain are worshipped, or devils."[1] Only when we know God's perfections—that He is the all-powerful, all-knowing, all-good Lord—do we see that He alone is worthy of our worship with all our hearts. Therefore, worshipers must be taught God's Word.

The Puritans also understood that we cannot approach God except through the Mediator, Jesus Christ. We have sinned against God. His presence is a consuming fire of holiness (Heb. 12:28–29). To draw near to Him, by the Spirit's grace, we must trust in Christ's blood and intercession to open the way for our acceptance (Heb. 10:19–22). Then we can worship the true God with a good conscience and great joy. Consequently, worship cannot be separated from preaching the gospel.

---

1. Perkins, *A Warning against the Idolatry of the Last Times, and an Instruction Touching Religious or Divine Worship*, in *Works*, 7:477.

The Regulative Principle of Worship

Since the goal of worship is to please God, the Puritans taught that the church must worship God only as God's Word commands. This is a distinctive of Reformed Christianity. Christians in most other traditions argue that we can add elements to God's worship if they do not contradict God's Word. However, the Puritans pointed out that the Holy Scriptures teach us to worship God as the Lord commanded (Ex. 25:9; 39:1), adding and subtracting nothing (Deut. 12:32), and not trusting our hearts or traditions to guide us (Num. 15:39; Ezek. 20:18; Matt. 15:9). God is not pleased with unauthorized "will worship," for it does not honor His holiness (Lev. 10:1–3).

There are some physical or external requirements for public worship, and the Puritans allowed for that. We meet in a building to keep the worshipers warm and dry but we must not think the building is a holy place. We wear appropriate clothing to cover our bodies but we must not think that clothing sets us apart as holy or makes us acceptable to God.

The focus of Puritan worship was not objects and ritual but the glory of God in Christ, hearing God's Word, praising God's name, praying for God's grace, and receiving God's blessing. Sermons were central to the whole service. Puritan pastors led their churches in substantial, heartfelt prayers for the needs of their members, the nation, and the advance of the gospel around the world. The Puritans loved to sing and found in the book of Psalms a divinely inspired hymnbook for the church of all times (Eph. 5:19; Col. 3:16). Monks and priests had sung the Psalms in Latin for centuries; the Reformation made the whole congregation into "a choir" and put the Psalms into the language of the common people. William Ames (1576–1652) commended the singing of the Psalms because "it brings a kind of sweet delight to godly minds," it enables "a more distinct and fixed meditation," and it results in more "mutual edification."[2]

The Sermon as the Center of Worship

Whereas the worship of the medieval church centered on visible images and ceremonial actions, the Puritans focused worship on the reading and the preaching of God's Word. Substantial portions of Scripture were read aloud to the congregation. The sermon was the highlight of the Puritan worship service. The sermon usually lasted about an hour and had several points of doctrine or teaching to believe and many "uses" or applications to put into practice. Church members

---

2. William Ames, *Conscience with the Power and Cases Thereof* (London: by E. G. for I. Rothwell, T. Slater, L. Blacklock, 1643), 2:43.

would often review and discuss the sermon's doctrines and applications between the services, and through the week in what they called "holy conference," that is, conversations with their families in family worship and with friends about the holy things of God. Richard Sibbes said, "Here is the benefit of holy conference and good speeches. One thing draws on another, and that draws another, till at last the soul be warmed and kindled with the consideration and meditation of heavenly things."[3] By encouraging each other through the week, the Puritans extended the worship of God so that all things become holy to the Lord.

---

3. Sibbes, "Bowels Opened," in *Works*, 2:133.

30

The Lord's Supper

The sacrament of the Lord's Supper was the topic of fierce debate during the Reformation. Roman Catholics insisted that the essence of the bread and wine was changed into the literal body and blood of Christ (transubstantiation). Lutheran Christians rejected that doctrine, but still taught that Christ is physically present in or with the elements of the Supper. Luther said that Christ was physically present "in, with, and under the bread," while the bread remained bread (consubstantiation). Others like Ulrich Zwingli said that the Supper is a mere memorial or remembrance of what Christ did. Some went so far as to say that such physical ceremonies were not important for spirituality. Reformed Christians, however, following Calvin's lead, believed that in the Lord's Supper, Christ is spiritually present to believers and is received by faith as "the true meat and drink of eternal life." According to the liturgies of the Reformed churches, Christ is received by lifting up our hearts "on high in heaven where Christ Jesus is our advocate at the right hand of His heavenly Father," and so we must not "cleave with our hearts unto the external bread and wine."[1] Jesus Christ comes down very low to meet His people at the level of their five senses (they hear the Word being proclaimed and they touch the bread, and see, smell, and taste the bread and wine), so that when they dwell by faith on Christ, He lifts up their hearts to sit and commune with Him in heavenly places.

The Puritans embraced the Reformed view of Holy Communion and found the Supper to be a rich opportunity to meet with the risen and ascended Christ. Stephen Charnock (1628–1680) said, "There is in this action more communion with God…than in any other religious act.… We have not so near a communion with a person…as we have by sitting with him at his table, partaking of the same bread and the same cup."[2] Dining with the Lord Jesus at His table, the

---

1. "Form for the Administration of the Lord's Supper," in *The Psalter* (Grand Rapids: Reformation Heritage Books, 2007), 139.
2. Charnock, *A Discourse of the End of the Lord's Supper*, in *Works*, 4:407.

Puritans celebrated the Lord's Supper as a foretaste of the wedding feast of the Lamb (Rev. 19:9).

The Elements of the Supper

Although the Lord's Supper was a spiritual feast with Christ, the Puritans recognized that it consisted of physical elements that we can touch and taste. Since we are not mere spirits but creatures of sense, God has given us the bread and the wine so that the unseen things of God's Word might be represented to us in a visible manner. However, the visible must not distract from the spiritual. Therefore, the Puritans purged the Lord's Supper of human additions and restored it to its basic biblical pattern so that Christ might be the center of attention. Just as believers eat the bread and drink the wine, so by faith they receive Christ and all His benefits, as they commune with Him.

Different churches celebrate the Supper in different ways, and the Puritans debated the proper method of its administration and reception. For most, it was important for the participants to sit at a table, as that most nearly resembles its original institution. For a few, the elements could be carried to people where they sat in the congregation. A few Puritan congregations celebrated the Supper every week, but most celebrated every two or three months.

Spiritual Partaking and Participants of the Lord's Supper

More important to the Puritans was the spiritual manner of partaking in the Supper. A few Puritans regarded the Lord's Supper as a converting sacrament and encouraged those earnestly seeking salvation to participate. The majority of Puritans, however, believed that only those who knew the basic truths of Christianity and professed saving faith in Christ should take the Supper.

None of the Puritans required full assurance of grace and salvation, though, for partaking of the Lord's Supper. "Weak and doubting Christians" were urged to partake. As Thomas Watson (c. 1620–1686) said, "A weak faith can lay hold of a strong Christ."[3] Then too, one of the major purposes of the Lord's Supper is to strengthen weak faith as believers eat and drink in remembrance of Christ.

Preparing for, Engaging in, and Reflecting upon the Supper

Since the Lord's Supper was the occasion for spiritual communion with the holy God, the Puritans called Christians to invest thought and feeling into it and avoid just going through the motions. They should prepare themselves by meditating

---

3. Thomas Watson, *The Lord's Supper* (Edinburgh: Banner of Truth, 2004), 73.

on Christ's death and examining themselves for faith, love, and obedience to Christ's commands.

Eating the bread and drinking the wine must be coupled with the active exercise of faith in Christ's finished work on the cross. John Owen said, "That which we are to endeavour in this ordinance is, to get…a view of Christ as lifted up; that is bearing our iniquities in his own body on the tree. O that God in this ordinance would give our souls a view of him!"[4] The partaker should apply Christ's blood to his spiritual needs for forgiveness, comfort, and sanctification.

After the service is over, the believer should reflect upon how Christ met with him and cherish the grace received. He should also go back into the world in the Lord's strength to live entirely for Him.

The Lord's Supper as a Holy Feast

The Puritans viewed the Lord's Supper as a sacred feast—a *remembrance* feast (hence the call of Jesus to "do this in remembrance of me" [1 Cor. 11:24]), a *strengthening* feast (to strengthen our weak faith), a *covenanting* feast (in which God and His people both covenant themselves to each other), a *love* feast (in which believers confess, "We love him, because he first loved us" [1 John 4:19]), and a *witnessing* feast (in which, by partaking, we confess to the entire church that Christ is our only hope for salvation). What a feast this holy Supper is when Christ is its center!

The Puritans also warned, however, against setting the Lord's Supper on a pedestal above the preaching of God's Word. On the other hand, they did acknowledge that sometimes Christ became particularly precious in Communion. But the "sacramental assurance," as they called it, was not something apart from and superior to the Word. Robert Bruce put it best when he said that we do not get a different Christ in the Supper than we do in the Word, even if sometimes we "get Him better in the Supper." The Lord's Supper is never to replace the Word but to supplement the Word—hence the Supper may not be administered independently from the preached Word.

Additional Spiritual Benefits from the Supper

What benefits did the Puritans expect from the Lord's Supper? The Supper confirms the faith of Christians in the saving death of Jesus Christ and increases their assurance. By faith, they receive fresh supplies of God's grace by union with Christ so that Christ refreshes them and reigns more powerfully in their lives.

---

4. Owen, "Sacramental Discourses," in *Works*, 9:582.

Communion not only presents a reminder to their minds, but also can stir their affections with love for Christ, hatred of sin, gratitude for God's mercy, and zeal to do His will.

Participation in this sacred meal is a distinguishing mark of the true church of Christ. It binds believers together as one, for they share one bread as a sign of union with one Christ. The rite also proclaims Christ to the world as unbelievers present in the congregation observe how central Christ and Him crucified is to the life of Christians. In many ways, the Supper glorifies Christ for it reveals Him and manifests His continuing presence with His church.

31

Church Offices and Government

Most people today give little thought to how their churches are governed and what the Bible says on this matter. Such was not the case in the sixteenth and seventeenth centuries. The Roman Catholic Church had long placed supreme earthly authority in the hands of the pope, making him Christ's "vicar" or representative on earth. Papal authority was extended through the clerical hierarchy of "prelates" of many kinds: cardinals, archbishops, bishops, canons, archdeacons, etc. When King Henry VIII separated the Church of England from the Roman papacy in 1534, authority in the church passed to the hands of the English monarch, the archbishops, and the bishops. Thus, the church was subjected to earthly "lords" who did not hesitate to employ coercive force to persecute those who would not conform to their doctrines, practices, and policies.

Church Offices

Though some Puritans continued to affirm the government of the church by bishops (episcopal government), most Puritans recognized that in the New Testament, the word translated "bishop" or "overseer" does not represent a distinct office of authority but is another term for "elder" (Acts 20:17, 28; Titus 1:5, 7). To set up a bishop or pope above the elders is to trespass into the office of the apostles who were "extraordinary ministers" with special authority and infallibility in doctrine. More importantly, it transgresses the authority of the Lord Jesus Christ, who alone is King and Head of the church. Christ alone has the right to reign over men's consciences and command their faith and worship.

According to common Puritan interpretation, there are two to four basic offices of authority in the church. Those who advocated four offices, like Calvin, distinguished the doctor or teacher (professor of theology) in the seminary or theological school from the minister of the Word in the local church, based on Ephesians 4:11 which refers to "pastors and teachers"—to which they added elders and deacons. Those who taught that there were three offices, which was the majority view, either combined the teaching office with the pastoral office, the ministers of the Word, to which they added elders and deacons, or they maintained a separate office of teacher and regarded the minister as an elder with a special calling to preach. A minority of Puritans believed in only two offices, namely, elders/overseers and deacons, based on Philippians 1:1 and 1 Timothy 3:1–13, with the elders taking on various specializations. For example, Laurence Chaderton said that some elders devote themselves to the ministry of the Word (1 Tim. 5:17). Of these ministers, some are "pastors" who primarily exhort people to holiness and administer the sacraments, and some are "teachers" who primarily educate people's minds in sound doctrine (Eph. 4:11). The remaining elders, though not ministers of the Word, play a crucial role in the government and discipline of the church because with the pastors and teachers they admonish the unruly and encourage the faithful. Deacons distribute the benevolent gifts of the church to help the poor, being assisted by women, especially widows.[1]

Church Government

The Puritans differed among themselves, however, as to how the elders exercised authority over Christ's churches. A vast majority of Puritans taught that synods or assemblies of elders had authority to rule over several congregations (presbyterian government). They argued that Acts 15 reveals the authority of a synod of elders over multiple churches. They also said that without a ruling synod, there would be no way to correct individual congregations that fell into error or oppressed their members. Synods represent the visible church in making common confession of the Christian faith. Presbyterian Puritans viewed the church as a visible kingdom with government and laws that transcend local congregations. Samuel Rutherford (1600–1661) said, "Christ…is a visible Head in this sense, in that he reigneth and ruleth, even in the external visible policy of his church, through all the catholic [universal] visible church, in his officers, lawful synods, [and] ordinances."[2]

Other Puritans—a small minority often called Independents—taught that there is no higher church authority than the local congregation as led by its own elders by its consent (congregational government). In this view, churches may fellowship with other churches and even hold synodical meetings among the elders of several churches. However, synods do not have binding authority over

---

1. Laurence Chaderton, *A Fruitfull Sermon, Vpon the 3. 4. 5. 6. 7. & 8. verses of the 12. Chapter of the Epistle of S. Paul to the Romanes* (London: Robert Walde-graue, 1584), 57, 61, 65–70.

2. Samuel Rutherford, *The Divine Right of Church-Government and Excommunication* (London: by John Field for Christopher Meredith, 1646), 18.

individual churches, at least not in weighty matters such as ordination of officers or excommunication of sinning members. Congregational Puritans emphasized that the church is a voluntary union of believers with one another, and its elders lead by the general consent of its members. Although the elders derive their authority directly from Christ and their direction from His Word, it is the nature of "the rule of the gospel," John Owen said, that the church's "obedience is voluntary and of choice."[3] In this manner, the church is unlike political kingdoms.

Puritans of both presbyterian and congregationalist persuasions avoided the extremes of sheer democracy (rule by popular vote) and sheer aristocracy (rule by an elite few) in the church. The Puritan approach to church government developed the concept of republican government in a manner that set a precedent for future representative democracies as in the North American colony of Massachusetts.

---

3. Owen, *A Brief Instruction in the Worship of God and Discipline of the Churches of the New Testament*, in *Works*, 15:501.

32

The Lord's Day

At the heart of Puritan worship was the Lord's Day. No other institution of worship receives specific mention in the Ten Commandments (Ex. 20:8–11). As the fourth commandment states, God instituted the Sabbath long before He gave the law to Israel. William Gouge (1575–1653) said that the Sabbath is part of God's moral law, that is, "a rule of life" that binds "all persons, in all places, at all times." We can see that this is so because God set apart the day as a holy day of rest at creation, when Adam represented all mankind before God, being the father of all nations, Jews and Gentiles (Gen. 2:2–3).[1] To be sure, the Jewish Sabbath had its legal peculiarities, but these faded away after Christ finished His redeeming work. However, Christ's taking of the Sabbath under His lordship (Mark 2:28), the church's observance of worship on the first day of the week (Acts 20:7; 1 Cor. 16:2), and the explicit reference to "the Lord's day" (Rev. 1:10) convinced the Puritans that setting apart the first day of the week exclusively for worshiping God was part of God's unchanging moral law—and continues as the Christian Sabbath.

The duties of the Lord's Day were divided, in typical Puritan analysis, into activities commanded, activities permitted, and activities forbidden. God commanded that people use the day to worship Him and engage in works of piety (Luke 4:16) and works of mercy (Mark 3:4).

Public Worship

Of course, Sabbatarian works of piety centered upon public worship with the gathered church. The Puritans gave much thought to dressing for church—not dressing their bodies but dressing their souls by spiritual preparation before arriving at the meeting house. Every sermon brought them closer either to heaven or to hell. Puritan pastors instructed their congregations in how to "take heed therefore how ye hear" the preaching of the Word (Luke 8:18).

---

1. William Gouge, *The Sabbaths Sanctification* (London: by G. M. for Joshua Kirton and Thomas Warren, 1641), 1.

The Whole Day as a Sabbath unto the Lord

However, the holiness of the Sabbath was far from exhausted in church services. George Swinnock (c. 1627–1673) said, "Reader, as thy duty is to rest the whole day from wickedness and worldly work, so also to employ the whole day in God's worship, be either praying, or reading, or hearing, or singing, or meditating, or discoursing with others about the works or word of God."[2] On this point, the Puritans stood upon Psalm 92, titled, "Song for the sabbath day," which calls for the declaration of the Lord's love in the morning and His faithfulness at night (v. 2). Whether God's works of creation or those of redemption, the glorious activity of the Lord provided the Puritans with ample material for meditation and adoration.

Works of mercy included visiting the suffering with practical help for body and soul, whether they were afflicted by illness, need, discouragement, doubt, or sin. God permitted works of necessity to meet the needs or remedy the weaknesses of ourselves and our households, for though those works are not holy in themselves, God is kind and tenderhearted. Activities forbidden by God on the Sabbath are the labors of our ordinary vocations, ordinary commerce in buying and selling, and recreations that would distract us from setting our hearts on the Lord. And, of course, sin is forbidden on all days, but it is aggravated when committed on the day that God set apart as holy.

Impact of the Lord's Day

The effects of the Reformed and Puritan Lord's Day upon the English nation (and later the United States of America) were astonishing. Keeping the Sabbath became engrained in British culture even among those who rejected Puritanism as a movement. Through the nineteenth century and well into the twentieth, it was common on the first day of the week for businesses to close, organized sports to cease, and people to give themselves to rest and worship.

Though Sabbath-keeping was mandated by divine law, the Puritans viewed it as more of a delight than a duty, more of an opportunity than merely an obligation. They considered the Lord's Day to be the "market day of the soul," as Thomas Watson said, the day to stock up on savory and nutritious food for one's spiritual life for the coming week.[3] Not only was it the day in history when Christ rose from the dead and later poured out the Holy Spirit at Pentecost—days of

---

2. Swinnock, *The Christian Man's Calling*, in *Works*, 1:245.
3. Watson, *A Body of Practical Divinity*, in *Works*, 278.

blessed memory—but it is the day the Lord appears in His holy temple, the living church. It is a day of glory and festival, a foretaste of the heavenly rest. There is much that we can learn from the Puritans about what it means to "call the sabbath a delight" (Isa. 58:13).[4]

---

4. See the classic Puritan work on Sabbath, Nicholas Bound (d. 1613), *The True Doctrine of the Sabbath* (repr., Grand Rapids: Reformation Heritage Books, 2016).

33

Preaching

The Puritan movement has been called a golden age of preaching. Through the preaching and the publication of sermons, the Puritans sought to reform the church and the everyday lives of people. With few exceptions, Puritan ministers were great preachers who lovingly and passionately proclaimed the whole counsel of God set forth in Holy Scripture. No group of preachers in church history has matched their biblical, doctrinal, experiential, and practical preaching. Four themes of Puritan preaching will be examined here: their view of the primacy of preaching, their passion for preaching, their power in preaching, and their plainness in preaching.

Primacy of Preaching

The Puritans had a profound conviction that God built His church primarily through the instrument of preaching. Preaching was central to their worship and devotion, first, because they believed the substance of preaching to be the declaring of God's Word to men. They were in awe that a mere man could be the mouthpiece and ambassador of the almighty, triune God.

Second, they saw preaching as God's great converting ordinance. It was the means by which God saved sinners—the Word was preached and people believed (1 Cor. 15:11).

Third, other than the gift of the Holy Spirit, the Puritans were convinced that the ascended Christ bestows no higher gift on His church than the call to preach. Richard Sibbes called it "a gift of all gifts."[1] Therefore, the Puritans put the pulpit rather than the altar at the center of their churches and put preaching rather than the sacraments at the center of their worship. Such a perspective made each sermon a momentous occasion.

---

1. Sibbes, "The Fountain Opened," in *Works*, 5:509.

Passion for Preaching

Puritan preaching was driven by an inward passion generated by the Spirit of God. They loved everything about proclaiming the gospel of Christ. Puritan ministers loved *preparing for preaching.* They spent long hours poring over the meaning of the text of Scripture with an eye to its application to their hearers.

Having prepared, Puritan preachers loved to *preach to themselves* first and foremost; they despised cold professionalism. The best sermons, they said, are those that the preacher first preaches to his own heart. Then, too, they loved the *act of preaching.* Samuel Rutherford said he had but "one joy" next to Christ, that is, "to preach Christ."[2]

Furthermore, the Puritans loved *the people they preached to* and relentlessly sought their conversion and edification. Puritan preachers understood that the minister with great preaching gifts who failed to love his people would fail miserably in his calling.

Power in Preaching

The Puritans believed that God would use their faithful preaching as a weapon to conquer sinners and build up saints. Their preaching addressed the *mind* with clarity. Believing knowledge to be the soil in which the Spirit planted the seed of regeneration, they informed the mind with biblical knowledge and reasoned with the mind through biblical logic. They understood that a mindless Christianity quickly fosters a spineless Christianity, and that an anti-intellectual gospel quickly becomes an empty, formless gospel that doesn't get beyond "felt needs."

Puritan preaching confronted the *conscience* pointedly. Preachers named specific sins, then asked questions to press home the guilt of those sins upon the consciences of their hearers in order to lead them to take refuge in Christ. They believed that ministers must go with the stick of divine truth and beat every bush behind which a sinner hides, until like Adam who hid, he stands before God in his nakedness.

Puritan preaching also allured the *heart* passionately. Their preaching was affectionate, zealous, and optimistic. In this way, they sought to powerfully affect the whole man with the whole of God's Word. They preached out of love for God's Word, love for the glory of God, and love for never-dying souls. They set forth Christ in His loveliness, moving their people to yearn to know Him better and live wholly for Him.

---

2. *Letters of Samuel Rutherford,* ed. Andrew Bonar (London: Oliphants, [1904?]), 420, 438 (letters of July 7 and 13, 1637).

Plainness in Preaching

In terms of style, the Puritans believed in a plain style of preaching. This plainness did not equate to anti-intellectualism but a simple and clear communication of truth from the Bible to the mind, then into the heart, and then outward to direct the conduct. Henry Smith said, "To preach simply, is not to preach unlearnedly, nor confusedly, but plainly and perspicuously [clearly], that the simplest which doth hear, may understand what is taught, as if he did hear his name."[3]

The first part of a Puritan sermon was exegetical and expositional, explaining the text of the sermon; the second, doctrinal and didactic, usually expounding one major doctrine drawn from the text; and the third, applicatory, which included both an emphasis on experiential preaching and discriminatory preaching.

For the Puritans, the applicatory part of preaching was the most important. The applicatory part is "the life of preaching," wrote James Durham (c. 1622–1658). "Hence, preaching is called persuading, testifying, beseeching, entreating, or requesting, exhorting."[4] These parts they often labelled as the "uses" of the text, which could become lengthy as the minister applied Scripture to various listeners. The goal always was to drive the Word of God home or, as Baxter put it, "to screw the truth into their minds, and work Christ into their affections."[5]

Puritan preaching was experiential and practical. Experiential preaching stresses the need to know by experience the truths of the Word of God. It seeks to explain in terms of biblical truth how matters *ought to go* and how they *do go* in the Christian life. It aims to apply divine truth to all of the believer's experience in his walk with God as well as his relationship with family, the church, and the world around him. We can learn much from the Puritans about this type of preaching.

These applications must target the right people or they might do more spiritual harm than good. Consequently, Puritan preaching was marked by a discriminating or discerning application of truth to the non-Christian and the Christian. Puritan preachers took great pains to identify the marks of grace that distinguish the church from the world, true believers from mere professing believers, and saving faith from temporary faith.[6] Thomas Shepard (*The Ten Virgins*),

---

3. Henry Smith, *Works of Henry Smith*, 2 vols. (Stoke-on-Trent, U. K.: Tentmaker Publications, 2002), 1:337.

4. James Durham, *A Commentary upon the Book of the Revelation* (Amsterdam: John Frederickszoon Stam, 1660), 260–66.

5. Richard Baxter, *The Reformed Pastor*, in *The Practical Works of Richard Baxter*, 4 vols. (London: George Virtue, 1838), 4:370.

6. Thomas Watson, *The Godly Man's Picture* (Edinburgh: Banner of Truth, 1992), 20–188, sets forth twenty-four marks of grace for self-examination.

Matthew Mead (*The Almost Christian Discovered*), Jonathan Edwards (*Religious Affections*), and other Puritans wrote dozens of works to differentiate imposters from true believers.[7]

Through application, Puritan preaching aimed to be transforming. The Puritans taught that when God's Word is preached experientially, the Holy Spirit uses it to transform individuals and nations.[8] Captain John Spilman provides us with an example of the transforming power of Puritan experiential preaching:

> Once in a carnal condition as I was, I did slight the Ministers of Christ, especially your long Preachers, and could not abide that any should preach long; but at last I was [caught] by one, and he was [preaching] on Hebrews 8:8, 10 [on] the new covenant made in Christ, which was applied to me very home, and touched me to the heart.[9]

The Puritan Preacher and His Preaching

To aim for the goal of transforming their hearers for the glory of God alone, the Puritans called preachers to conduct themselves in the fear of the Lord. The preacher must walk in humility, not flaunting his abilities, but possessing a keen awareness of his inability to bring anyone to Christ. They were convinced that both preacher and listener are totally dependent on the work of the Spirit to effect regeneration in whom He will.

Therefore, ministers must give themselves to prayer—prayer for themselves, for their hearers, for the church, and for God's glory. In this way, the Puritans did not place their confidence in the preacher, nor in the sermon itself, but rather in the Lord who used the faithful proclamation of His Word to advance His cause in the earth.

---

7. Thomas Shepard, *The Parable of the Ten Virgins* (Ligonier, Pa.: Soli Deo Gloria, 1990); Matthew Mead, *The Almost Christian Discovered; Or the False Professor Tried and Cast* (Ligonier, Pa.: Soli Deo Gloria, 1988); Jonathan Edwards, *Religious Affections* (New Haven, Conn.: Yale University Press, 1959).

8. Cf. Tae-Hyeun Park, *The Sacred Rhetoric of the Holy Spirit: A Study of Puritan Preaching in Pneumatological Perspective* (Proefschrift: Theologische Universiteit Apeldoorn, 2005), 373–74.

9. John Spilman, *A Tabernacle for the Sun*, 4, quoted in Owen C. Watkins, *The Puritan Experience: Studies in Spiritual Autobiography* (New York: Schocken, 1972), 58.

34

Listening to Sermons

The Puritans offered practical direction on how to listen to the preaching of God's Word.[1] The Westminster Larger Catechism (Q. 160) summarizes their advice as follows: "It is required of those that hear the word preached, that they attend upon it with diligence, preparation, and prayer, examine what they hear by the Scriptures, receive the truth with faith, love, meekness, and readiness of mind, as the word of God; meditate, and confer of it in their hearts, and bring forth the fruit of it in their lives."[2] In this answer, the Puritans offer help in three areas: how to prepare for the preached Word, how to receive the preached Word, and how to practice the preached Word.

Preparing for the Preached Word

1. Before beginning the Lord's Day, *prepare* to lay aside your day-to-day concerns, and take up the great work of the "market day of the soul."[3] The Puritans said preparation for worship should start on Saturday evening. Just as people baked bread on Saturday evening so it would be fresh on Sunday morning, so people should study the Word on Saturday evenings so that their hearts would be fresh—and like freshly baked bread, warm—for worship on Sunday. Before coming to God's house to hear His Word, prepare yourself and your family *with prayer*. The Puritans said we should dress our bodies for worship and our souls with prayer.

---

1. Samuel Annesley, "How May We Give Christ a Satisfying Account [of] Why We Attend upon the Ministry of the Word?," in *Puritan Sermons 1659–1689*, 4:173–98; David Clarkson, "Hearing the Word," in *The Works of David Clarkson*, 3 vols. (Edinburgh: Banner of Truth, 1988), 1:428–46; Watson, *A Body of Practical Divinity*, in *Works*, 359–61, 377–80; Thomas Boston, *An Illustration of the Doctrines of the Christian Religion*, in *The Complete Works of the Late Rev. Thomas Boston*, ed. Samuel M'Millan, 12 vols. (Wheaton, Ill.: Richard Owen Roberts, 1980), 2:427–54.
2. *Westminster Confession of Faith* (Glasgow: Free Presbyterian Publications, 1997), 253.
3. See James T. Dennison, Jr., *The Market Day of the Soul: The Puritan Doctrine of the Sabbath in England, 1532–1700* (Morgan, Pa.: Soli Deo Gloria, 2001).

2. Come with a *hearty appetite* for the Word. A good appetite promotes good digestion and growth. Peter encouraged spiritual appetite, saying, "As newborn babes, desire the sincere milk of the word, that ye may grow thereby" (1 Peter 2:2). The key Puritan word here is "diligence." The Sabbath is the great day of the week, and the hearing of the Word of God is the greatest privilege of the day. It takes much forethought and care, much clearing of agendas and focusing of the mind and heart, to make the best use of the day, and to profit the most from the Word preached.

3. Meditate on *the importance of the preached Word* as you enter God's house. The high and holy triune God of heaven and earth is meeting with you to speak directly to you. Thomas Boston wrote, "The voice is on earth, [but] the speaker is in heaven" (Acts 10:33).[4] The Puritans taught that the preached gospel will either lift us up to heaven or cast us down to hell. "The nearer to heaven any are lifted up by gospel preaching, the lower will they sink into hell if they heed it not," wrote David Clarkson.[5]

4. Remember as you enter the house of God that *you are entering a battleground.* Many enemies will oppose your listening, the Puritans said. You may be distracted by worldly cares and employments, lusts of the flesh, cold hearts, and critical spirits. With might and main Satan opposes your listening to God's Word. When you are tempted during worship by Satan, Samuel Annesley advises that you rebuke him, saying, "Be gone, Satan! I will parley no longer. If others neglect salvation, therefore must I? Will their missing of salvation relieve me for the loss of mine? Through Christ, I defy you."[6]

5. Finally, come with a *loving, expectant faith* (Ps. 62:1, 5). Thomas Watson advised that you attend the sermon swift to hear, slow to speak, and determined, like Mary, to keep and ponder God's Word in your heart. Come pleading God's promise that His Word will not return to Him void (Isa. 55:10–11).

Receiving the Preached Word

1. Listen with *an understanding, tender conscience.* Jesus's parable of the sower (Matt. 13:3–23; Mark 4:1–20; Luke 8:4–15) presents us with four types of listeners:

---

4. Boston, *An Illustration of the Doctrines of the Christian Religion*, in *Works*, 2:428.
5. Clarkson, "Hearing the Word," in *Works*, 1:430–31.
6. Annesley, "Ministry of the Word," in *Puritan Sermons 1659–1689*, 4:187.

the stonyhearted, superficial listener; the easily impressed but resistant listener; the half-hearted, distracted listener; and the understanding, fruitful listener. Make sure you belong to the last category, the Puritans said, which brings forth fruit, "some an hundredfold, some sixty, some thirty" (Matt. 13:23).

2. Listen with *submissive faith*. As James 1:21 says, "Receive with meekness the engrafted word." This kind of meekness, Watson said, involves a submissive frame of heart, "a willingness to hear the counsels and reproofs of the word." Through this kind of faith, the Word is engrafted into the soul and produces "the sweet fruit of righteousness."[7] Faith is the key to profitably receiving the Word. "The whole Word is the object of faith," wrote Thomas Manton. Therefore we need:

> faith in the histories, for our warning and caution; faith in the doctrines, to increase our reverence and admiration; faith in the threatenings, for our humiliation; faith in the precepts, for our subjection; and faith in the promises, for our consolation. They all have their use: the histories to make us wary and cautious; the doctrines to enlighten us with a true sense of God's nature and will; the precepts to direct us, and to try and regulate our obedience; the promises to cheer and comfort us; the threatenings to terrify us, to run anew to Christ, to bless God for our escape, and to add spurs to our duty.[8]

3. Listen with *humility and serious self-examination*. Do I humbly examine myself under the preaching of God's Word, trembling at its impact (Isa. 66:2)? Do I relish having the Word of God applied to my life? Do I pray that the Spirit may apply His Word, as Robert Burns put it, to my "business and bosom"?[9]

Practicing the Preached Word
1. *Strive to retain and pray over what you have heard.* Hebrews 2:1 says, "We ought to give the more earnest heed to the things which we have heard, lest at any time we should let them slip." Thomas Watson said we should not let sermons run through our minds like water through a sieve. "Our memories should be like the chest of the ark, where the law was put,"[10] he wrote. Joseph Alleine said one way to remember the preached Word is to "come from your knees to

---

7. Watson, *Body of Practical Divinity*, in *Works*, 360.
8. Thomas Manton, *The Life of Faith* (Ross-shire, Scotland: Christian Focus, 1997), 223–24.
9. Robert Burns, introduction to *The Works of Thomas Halyburton* (London: Thomas Tegg, 1835), xiv.
10. Watson, *Body of Practical Divinity*, in *Works*, 360.

the sermon, and come from the sermon to your knees."[11] Careful note-taking is a help in this duty; not a few Puritan sermons were preserved and later published from the notes taken by those who heard them.

2. *Familiarize yourself with the truths you have heard.* The Westminster Directory for Public Worship advises parents to engage in "repetition of sermons, especially by calling their families to an account of what they have heard."[12] When you come home from church, the Puritans advised, speak to your loved ones about the sermon you have heard in an edifying, practical manner.

3. *Put the sermon into action.* The Puritans taught that a sermon is not over when the minister says "Amen." Rather, that is when the final part of the sermon begins. In an old Scottish story, a wife asked her husband if the sermon was done when he arrived home. "No," he replied, "It has been said, but it has yet to be done." James 1:22 tells us, "Be ye doers of the word, and not hearers only, deceiving your own selves." Of what value is a mind filled with knowledge when it is not matched with a fruitful life?

4. *Lean upon the Holy Spirit.* Beg God to accompany His Word with the effectuating blessing of the Holy Spirit (Acts 10:44). As the Westminster divines put it, that the Spirit will make the Word "effectual to salvation" (Larger Catechism, Q. 155). If these directions are ignored, the preached Word will lead to our condemnation. As Thomas Watson wrote: "The word will be effectual one way or the other; if it does not make your hearts better, it will make your chains heavier.... Dreadful is their case who go loaded with sermons to hell."[13]

"Take heed therefore how ye hear" (Luke 8:18)!

---

11. Joseph Alleine, *A Sure Guide to Heaven* (Edinburgh: Banner of Truth, 1999), 29.
12. *Westminster Confession of Faith*, 386.
13. Watson, *Body of Practical Divinity*, in *Works*, 361.

35

Pastoral Counseling

The Puritans were master physicians of the soul. They referred to biblical counseling as *casuistry*. By *casuistry* they meant the light of moral theology applied with biblical integrity to various "cases of conscience" that a person is confronted with in his faith or walk. It is practical theology, training Christians to live uprightly, humbly, and joyfully in the presence of God every day of their lives. William Perkins and his successor, William Ames, were pioneers in developing Puritan casuistry biblically, systematically, and comprehensively. Standing upon their shoulders, the subsequent generations of English Puritans built upon their work, leaving a rich legacy of the application of biblical truth to the various conditions and struggles of the soul.

Let's look briefly at the setting, balance, means, focus, and goal of Puritan counseling.

The Setting

For the Puritans, biblical counseling began in and was primarily done from the pulpit. As Ken Sarles says, "Puritan preaching constituted a form of preventative counseling, as the truths of Scripture were applied to the conscience."[1]

The Puritans followed up pulpit counseling with private visitation, soul-counseling, and catechizing in the home. Richard Baxter said many people "who have been so long unprofitable hearers, have got more knowledge and remorse of conscience in half an hour's close disclosure, than they did from ten years' public preaching."[2] Baxter and his assistants spent two full days each week visiting parishioners in their homes. Those visits involved patiently teaching, examining, and leading families to Christ through the Scriptures.

---

1. Ken L. Sarles, "The English Puritans: A Historical Paradigm of Biblical Counseling," in John MacArthur, Wayne A. Mack, and the Master's College Faculty, *Introduction to Biblical Counseling: A Basic Guide to the Principles and Practice of Counseling* (Nashville, Tenn.: Thomas Nelson, 1994), 26.
2. Baxter, *The Reformed Pastor*, in *Works*, 4:443.

The Balance

While the Puritans stressed the need to listen to those whom they were counseling, they also warned that we "must not be too curious in prying into the weakness of others."[3] When that route is taken, they said a troubled person tends to become too dependent on the counselor. Unlike many modern psychoanalysts, they believed counseling should be directive, offering teaching on what to do and how to do it as a believer.

Puritan casuistic literature is devoted to answering a massive variety of significant questions. These include how to pray, how to meditate, how to gain an awakened and assured conscience, how to behave in the family, how to be a father, how to be a mother, how to be a God-fearing child, how to think through problems in the community, and how to apply biblical directives to decision making. The Puritans believed that the credible pastor-counselor is one who listens well, who encourages a troubled person to divulge his problems, then counsels the person scripturally, practically, faithfully, and realistically on how to live.

The Means

The great means of counseling, according to the Puritans, are the Word of Christ and prayer to the Father, both done in the Holy Spirit. They believed in the sufficiency of Scripture for diagnosing and remedying the various soul-struggles of men. Man's great problem is sin and his great need is Christ. John Owen wrote, "The daily exercise of faith on Christ as crucified…is the great fundamental means of mortification of sin in general."[4]

The Puritans would thus wield the gospel against a whole host of spiritual diseases. And they did this in a posture of prayer, knowing that God alone could change the hearts of their people. If the Spirit did not take their biblical counsel and apply it to the minds, wills, and affections of their hearers, then no true change would occur. For counseling to be fruitful, it must radically depend upon God and His Word.

The Focus

The Puritan counselor was not primarily worried about a person's self-esteem. He was far more concerned about the person's relationship to the triune God. That is not to say that self-esteem is not important in certain aspects of life—for

---

3. Sibbes, *The Bruised Reed and Smoking Flax*, in *Works*, 1:57.
4. Owen, *A Treatise of the Dominion of Sin and Grace*, in *Works*, 7:527.

example, a person must have some self-esteem and confidence to be able to do his work faithfully and well, but self-esteem counsel that does not center ultimately upon the triune God and His grace is seriously flawed, the Puritans would say.

The Puritans understood that apart from God's grace, we are fallen, wretched, unworthy, and hell-bound. Therefore, God-centeredness, not self-centeredness, is the key to a healthy self-image. They understood that when a person is rightly related to God in Christ, he will be rightly related to self.

The Goal
By their counseling the Puritans sought the sanctification and eternal welfare of their people. They did not look for quick and easy conversions; they were committed to building up lifelong believers whose hearts, minds, wills, and affections were won to the service of Christ, grounded on the Word of God, and filled with His Spirit.

The glorification of God through the holiness of His people motivated Puritan counseling. They used the means which God had prescribed with a confident expectation that God would build His kingdom among men.

36

Evangelism

Evangelism was not a word the Puritans commonly used, but they were evangelists nonetheless. Richard Baxter's *Call to the Unconverted* and Joseph Alleine's *Alarm to the Unconverted* were pioneer works in evangelistic literature. For these and other Puritans, evangelism was a Word-centered task of the church, particularly of her ministers. They were to be "fishers of men," seeking to awaken the unconverted to their need of Christ, to lead them to faith and repentance, and to establish them in a lifestyle of sanctification.

Let's look at Puritan evangelism from four perspectives: the message, method, disposition of the evangelist, and faithfulness.

The Message

Puritan evangelism was *thoroughly biblical*. A typical page of a Puritan evangelistic sermon contains five to ten citations of biblical texts and about a dozen references to additional texts. They used the whole Bible to confront the whole man. Puritan ministers did not merely pressure the human will to respond on the basis of a few texts that emphasize the volitional aspect of evangelism. Certainly, the duty to respond to the gospel in faith is important, but so are other duties. There is the duty to repent—not just as a temporary feeling of sorrow, but as a full amendment of life. The Puritans preached the law before the gospel, believing that through a confrontation with the demands of the law, the Holy Spirit would bring sinners to know their helplessness before God and their need of salvation.

Puritan evangelism was *unashamedly doctrinal*. They proclaimed God's majestic being, His trinitarian personality, and His glorious attributes. All of their evangelism was rooted in robust, biblical teaching about God in His three glorious persons. They likewise proclaimed the doctrine of Christ. "Preaching is the chariot that carries Christ up and down the world," wrote Richard Sibbes.[1]

---

1. Sibbes, *The Fountain Opened*, in *Works*, 5:508.

Puritan evangelists repeatedly presented Christ in His power and willingness to save, and in His preciousness as the only Redeemer of lost sinners. They did so with theological articulation, divine grandeur, and human passion. Preaching the whole Christ to the whole man, Puritan evangelists offered Him as Prophet, Priest, and King. They did not separate His benefits from His person or offer Him as a Savior from sin while ignoring His claims as Lord.

The Method

The Puritans employed two primary methods of evangelism. First, *plain preaching*. The Puritan "plain style of preaching" avoided all that was not perspicuous (i.e., clear) to an ordinary listener. William Perkins wrote that preaching "must be plain, perspicuous, and evident…the plainer, the better."[2] They used the plain style of preaching because they were evangelistic to the core—they wanted to reach everyone so that all might know the way of salvation.

Second, *catechetical teaching*. Scores of Puritans reached out evangelistically to children and young people by writing catechism books that explained fundamental Christian doctrines via questions and answers supported by Scripture. For example, John Cotton titled his catechism *Milk for Babes*.

At various levels in the church as well as in the homes of their parishioners, Puritan ministers catechized in order to explain the fundamental teachings of the Bible, to help people understand and examine their spiritual condition and to encourage them to flee to Christ, to help young people commit the Bible to memory, to make sermons and the sacraments more understandable and profitable, to enhance family worship, to prepare covenant children for confession of faith, to teach them how to defend their faith against error, and to help parents teach their own children.[3]

The Puritans viewed catechizing as a follow-up to sermons and a way to reach neighbors with the gospel. Joseph Alleine reportedly followed up his work on Sunday five days a week by catechizing church members as well as reaching out with the gospel to people he met on the streets.[4]

The hard work of the Puritan catechist was greatly rewarded. Due to close discipleship being carried on through catechizing, together with the Spirit's blessing,

2. Perkins, *Commentary on Galatians*, in *Works*, 2:148.
3. Cf. W. G. T. Shedd, *Homiletics and Pastoral Theology* (London: Banner of Truth, 1965), 356–75; J. Lewis Wilson, "Catechisms, and Their Use among the Puritans," in *One Steadfast High Intent* (London: Puritan and Reformed Studies Conference, 1966), 38–42.
4. Charles Stanford, *Joseph Alleine: His Companions and Times* (London: Jackson, Walford, and Hodder, 1861), 144–47.

Baxter could say at the end of his ministry that of the six hundred converts that were brought to faith under his preaching at Kidderminster, in Worcestershire, he could not name one that had backslidden to the ways of the world.

The Disposition of the Evangelist

The Puritan evangelist brought to his work a unique inward disposition or frame of mind and soul. There are two inner characteristics which are particularly noteworthy.

First, the Puritans *showed a profound dependence upon the Holy Spirit in their evangelism.* They felt keenly their inability to bring anyone to Christ, as well as the magnitude of conversion in depth and scope. "God never laid it upon thee to convert those he sends thee to. No; to publish the gospel is thy duty," William Gurnall said to ministers.[5] The Puritans were convinced that both preacher and listener are totally dependent on the work of the Spirit to effect regeneration and conversion when, how, and in whom He will. The Spirit brings God's presence into human hearts. He persuades sinners to seek salvation, renews corrupt wills, and makes scriptural truths take root in stony hearts.

Second, the Puritans *saturated all their evangelistic efforts in prayer.* They were "men of the closet" first of all. They were great evangelists only because they were also great petitioners who wrestled with God for divine blessing upon their gospel preaching. Baxter said, "Prayer must carry on our work as well as preaching; he preacheth not heartily to his people, that prayeth not earnestly for them. If we prevail not with God to give them faith and repentance, we shall never prevail with them to believe and repent."[6]

The Faithfulness

The Puritans were devoted to the declaration of the entire economy of redemption by focusing on the saving work of all three persons of the Trinity, while simultaneously calling sinners to a life of faith and commitment, and warning that the gospel will condemn forever those who persist in unbelief and impenitence. They displayed a profound faithfulness to Christ in their evangelistic message and method—and that was on display through their disposition.

---

5. William Gurnall, *The Christian in Complete Armour*, 2 vols. in 1 (repr., London: Banner of Truth, 1964), 2:574.
6. Baxter, *The Reformed Pastor*, in *Works*, 4:393.

PART SIX

Puritans in Daily Life

37

Meditation and Prayer

The Puritans were intimately acquainted with God. In addition to reading Scripture and listening to sermons, two primary means by which they sought to cultivate an ever-deepening communion with God were the biblical disciplines of meditation and prayer.

Puritan Meditation

The word *meditate* means to "think upon" or "reflect." The Puritans never tired of saying that biblical meditation involves thinking upon the triune God and His Word. By anchoring meditation in the living Word, Jesus Christ, and God's written Word, the Bible, the Puritans distanced themselves from mysticism—which stresses contemplation at the expense of action, and unrestrained imagination at the expense of biblical content. They called meditation the halfway house between Scripture reading (or listening to scriptural sermons) and prayer. In other words, meditation is the believer's tool to glean the most benefit or profit—through recall and reflection—from the Word read and heard, and then to apply that new, fuller understanding of God and self to prayer.

The Puritans practiced and wrote extensively about two kinds of meditation: occasional and deliberate. In *occasional meditation* the believer makes use of what he sees with his eyes or hears with his ears to direct him to the contemplation of heavenly matters. That's what David did with the moon and stars in Psalm 8, what Solomon did with the ants in Proverbs 6, and what Christ did with well water in John 4. But the most important kind of meditation is daily, *deliberate meditation*, engaged in at set times. Such meditation prayerfully ponders a biblical text or truth in its application to all of life.

For the Puritans, meditation exercised both the mind and the heart; he who meditates approaches a subject with his intellect as well as his affections. Edmund Calamy wrote, "A true meditation is when a man doth so meditate of Christ as to get his heart inflamed with the love of Christ; so meditate of the

Truths of God, as to be transformed into them."[1] They believed that for meditation to be fruitful it must enter three doors: the door of understanding, the door
of the heart and affections, and the door of practical living—the working out of
the Word in daily life.

Meditation was believed to be a daily duty that enhanced every other duty
of the Christian life. As oil lubricates an engine, so meditation facilitates the dili-
gent use of the means of grace, deepens the marks of grace, and strengthens one's
relationships to others. This led Thomas Brooks to write, "It is not he that reads
most; but he that meditates most, that will prove the choicest, sweetest, wisest,
and strongest Christian."[2] And such meditation, in particular, produced men and
women of powerful or "effectual fervent prayer" (James 5:16).

Puritan Prayer

The Puritans were truly "men of the closet." In their closets—their special, private place dedicated to prayer—they would cry aloud to the God of heaven for
divine benediction upon themselves, their ministries, families, churches, and
nation. They delighted in prayer as a holy communication between heaven and
the believing soul.

True prayer, said the Puritans, is *varied in its expression*. They recognized that
the Scriptures present various kinds of prayer: praise of God's glories, confession
of sin, petition for needs, thanks for God's mercies, intercession for others, and
assertions of confidence that God is willing and able to answer. They maintained
balance in their praying by making Scripture the content of their prayers.

True prayer is marked by *sincerity and affection toward God*. To pray with
the mouth what is not truly in the heart is hypocrisy—unless one is confessing
the coldness of his heart and crying out for heartwarming grace. Brooks writes,
"There is no prayer acknowledged, approved, accepted, recorded, or rewarded by
God, but that wherein the heart is sincerely and wholly."[3]

True prayer is *grounded in God's promises*. The Puritans made much of praying God's promises back to Him. William Gurnall wrote, "Prayer is nothing but
the promise reversed, or God's Word formed into an argument, and retorted
by faith upon God again."[4] In His sovereignty, God has bound Himself by the

1. Edmund Calamy, *The Art of Divine Meditation* (London: for Tho. Parkhurst, 1634), 26–28.
2. Thomas Brooks, *Precious Remedies against Satan's Devices*, in *The Complete Works of Thomas Brooks*, ed. Alexander Balloch Grosart, 6 vols. (Edinburgh: James Nichol, 1866–1867), 1:8.
3. Brooks, *The Privy Key of Heaven*, in *Works*, 2:256–57.
4. Gurnall, *The Christian in Complete Armour*, 2:88.

promises He has made to His church. If Christians would be effective, they must show God His own handwriting in prayer.

True prayer is *sustained by the assistance of the Holy Spirit.* The Puritans emphasized that without the Spirit, the prayers of God's people are mere empty words; but with Him, prayer becomes the effectual unbosoming of the heart to God. The Spirit of God touches the wellspring of the affections, provoking and stirring up prayer within His people. Having his heart affected in such a way by the Spirit, the believer cannot but pour out his desires to God in a manner consistent with Scripture and pleasing to God.

Inseparable Connection

According to the Puritans, meditation and prayer were inseparably related. Meditation is carried out in a spirit of prayer, acknowledging that God alone can open the eyes of the understanding to grasp His truth. And effectual prayers are those offered by a mind *saturated* with the truth, affections *elevated by the application* of the truth, and a will *conformed* to the truth, all of which are the fruits of biblical meditation. By these twin disciplines, they sought growth in the grace and knowledge of Christ.

38

Conscience

When the Puritan Richard Rogers and one of his neighbors were riding horses, the neighbor commented, "I like you and your company very well, only you are too precise." Rogers explained why. "O sir," he said, "I serve a precise God!"[1] He could not be any less precise in obedience to God's Word than God was in His commanding. Such a conviction was the fruit of a good conscience before God, something which the Puritans saw as central to a life of godliness.

The Nature of Conscience

According to the Puritans, the conscience is a universal aspect of human nature by which God has established His authority in the soul for men to judge themselves rationally. The apostle Paul describes conscience as "the work of the law written in their hearts" (Rom. 2:14–15). Both Scripture and experience affirm that every person has a conscience. Those who deny the existence of a conscience are motivated more by their sin than their principles. Most Puritan theologians defined conscience as a rational faculty that provides moral self-knowledge and moral judgment concerning right and wrong. William Ames described it as "a man's judgment of himself according to the judgment of God on him."[2] They understood the conscience to function as a spiritual nervous system, which uses guilt to inform us that something is wrong and needs correction. Normally the judgment of conscience is supreme, impartial, faithful, and private, William Fenner said. He went on to say, "Ye need not go far to know what state you are in: there is that in your bosom that can decide the matter."[3]

---

1. The anecdote is related by Giles Firmin, *The Real Christian, or a Treatise of Effectual Calling* (London: for Dorman Newman, 1670), 67.

2. Ames, *Conscience with the Power and Cases Thereof*, 1:2.

3. William Fenner, *The Souls Looking-Glasse, Lively Representing Its Estate before God with a Treatise of Conscience* (Cambridge: by Roger Daniel, for John Rothwell, 1643), 12.

The Corruption of Conscience

The conscience, however, was profoundly affected by man's fall into sin and misery. When the conscience is not good, it can prompt actions and reasonings that are unscriptural and unreliable. The Puritans wrote a great deal about various types of evil consciences.

- *The trembling or doubting conscience* accuses the soul of sin and threatens the soul with God's wrath and the expectation of death and judgment. This type of conscience is evil as long as it does not drive its owner to Jesus Christ for salvation.

- *The moralist conscience* exercises outwardly moral virtues and good works, but it falls far short in God's book of reckoning. It can never do any real, abiding, spiritual good, for it does not operate by saving faith and thus does not serve God's glory.

- *The scrupulous conscience* makes much out of religious duties and moral trifles but does not look to Christ alone for salvation nor find peace in Christ. It engages in the kind of Christ-less self-examination that produces aimless introspection and inner gloom.

- *The erring conscience* includes various forms of ignorance and misperception because it wrongly applies God's Word. Samuel Annesley explains, "Conscience, evil informed, takes human traditions and false doctrines, proposed under the show of Divine authority to be the will of God."[4]

- *The drowsy conscience* is that of every unconverted person who is not yet facing the reality of their impending doom. This makes them indifferent to their impending death and judgment and unmoved by the horrors of hell.

- *The seared conscience* is the worst of all, putting people beyond the hope of salvation. This enables the sinner to "swallow down sin like drink… without any remorse."[5] It is God's greatest judgment this side of hell.

---

4. Annesley, "How May We Be Universally and Exactly Conscientious?," in *Puritan Sermons 1659–1689*, 1:13.

5. Fenner, *The Souls Looking-Glasse*, 85.

The Restoration of Conscience

In God's restoration of His image in the soul, He also restores the conscience. The Puritans taught that, first, the conscience must be *awakened by preaching*. They were not content to merely teach doctrine clearly but sought to pierce the consciences of men with the Word to show them what was at the bottom of their hearts.

Second, the conscience must be *informed by Scripture*. For the Puritan, conscience is the faculty that God puts in us to be a sounding board for applying His Word to our lives. Our consciences should be educated by what is taught in Scripture and trained to judge according to Scripture. Then the voice of conscience will be the voice of God indeed.

Conscience, third, must be *healed by the gospel*. A good conscience finds peace through the gospel and its promises. God's promises are the means by which peace, pardon, acceptance, reconciliation to God, and affection between God and a person nurture and protect the conscience. According to the Puritans, one of the most blessed things in the world is to have a good conscience through the application of such promises.

Finally, the conscience must be *exercised by self-examination*. This entails asking yourself questions to help you see how your life measures against the moral law of God.

Conclusion: A Word-Bound Conscience

By its very nature, conscience must be active. But the Puritans understood that a good conscience acts out of knowledge of God's Word, promoting both scriptural obedience and scriptural liberty rather than legalism or carelessness about sin. Conscience can only serve us reliably as an inner pilot when it is aided by the "chart and compass" of the Word and Spirit of God.

39

Marriage

The Puritans had a refreshingly biblical and positive view of marriage. Building on Reformation teaching, they set forth the scriptural purposes and principles for marriage, as well as practices of marriage.

Purposes for Marriage

The Puritans believed that Scripture identifies three purposes for marriage, all of which aim for the glory of God and the furthering of God's kingdom on earth. The first purpose for marriage is to provide companionship and mutual assistance. Through such companionship, William Perkins says, "the parties married may perform the duties of their callings in [a] better and more comfortable manner (Prov. 31:11–13)."[1]

The second purpose of marriage is procreation and the building up of the church through godly child-rearing. The Puritans viewed children as a gift of God through which believers are to serve the family, the church, and the state.

The third purpose of marriage, as Gouge says, is to allow men and women to "possess their vessels in holiness and honor" (cf. 1 Thess. 4:4) and to avoid fornication (1 Cor. 7:2, 9).[2] Marriage is the best and most sanctified antidote to the lusts of the flesh.

Principles for Marriage

The Puritans understood marriage in terms of two major scriptural principles: the Christ-church principle and the covenantal principle. These principles are perhaps the primary factors behind the orderliness, stability, and happiness of Puritan marriages.

---

1. Perkins, *Christian Oeconomie: or, A Short Survey of the Right Manner of Erecting and Ordering a Family, according to the Scriptures*, in *Works*, 10:125.
2. William Gouge, *Of Domesticall Duties* (London: by John Haviland for William Bladen, 1622), 209–10.

The Christ-church principle. The Puritans embraced the biblical teaching that the husband is to love his wife as Christ loves the church, while the wife is to show reverence and submission to her husband as the church does to Christ. The husband must love his wife absolutely, purposefully, realistically, and sacrificially (Eph. 5:25–29). Modeling the husband's headship on Christ's headship of the church, Puritans understood that male authority was more a charge to loving responsibility than a ticket to privilege. Similarly, the wife's submission to her husband means that she should show reverence and "yield subjection" to her husband in all things, except when her husband acts contrary to God and His commandments.[3]

One of the most biblically radical Puritan ideas about the Christ-church principle of marriage is that the focus of both husband and wife in marriage should be on his or her own duties, not on whether or not the other is fulfilling his or her duties. In other words, a husband is to treat his wife as Christ treats the church regardless of how his wife is fulfilling her God-given duties, and a wife is to respect and show submission to her husband as the church shows to Christ regardless of her husband's faithfulness to his God-given duties.

The covenantal principle. Flowing out of this principle of love and submission, the Puritans made much of the principle of marriage as a covenant (Mal. 2:14). Both parties in a marriage freely and voluntarily consent to live according to the rules of marriage which God set when He solemnized the union of our first parents. When a man and a woman enter into holy matrimony before the Lord, they promise to fulfil the duties of marriage without conditions and without reservations. "Therefore," writes Samuel Willard, "when husband and wife neglect their duties they not only wrong each other, but they provoke God by breaking his law."[4]

Practices of Marriage
The Puritans let the practices, duties, and ethics of marriage flow out of the marriage textbook of Scripture. They classified the duties of the marital union under three headings: mutual duties, the husband's duties, and the wife's duties.

---

3. Isaac Ambrose, *The Practice of Sanctification*, in *Works of Isaac Ambrose* (London: by Fisher, Son, & Co., for Thomas Tegg, & Son, 1835), 133.
4. Quoted in Morgan, *The Puritan Family*, 30.

Mutual duties. The foundational duty of marriage is love. Gouge writes, "A loving mutual affection must pass betwixt husband and wife, or else no duty will be well performed: this is the ground of all the rest."[5] From this love, a husband and wife must be faithful to each other and help each other in every conceivable way, including seeking each other's spiritual growth, praying for one another, cultivating true friendship, promoting each other's reputation, and working diligently as a team. In short, this love must be spiritual (fearing and loving God above all), superlative (loving each other more than anyone else on earth), and physical (enjoying each other intimately [i.e., sexually] to God's glory). This emphasis on full-orbed love and romance within marriage (rather than in extramarital relations, as was common in the Middle Ages), is a gift the Puritans have bequeathed to us. Herbert Richardson correctly notes that "the rise of romantic marriage and its validation by the Puritans represents a major innovation within the Christian tradition."[6]

The husband's duties. The Puritans taught that in addition to loving his wife and fulfilling mutual marital duties, the husband must govern his wife—not tyrannically, but as an equal, exercising leadership, not lordship. Husbands should delight in their wives, esteeming them, respecting them, and seeking to please them. Then, too, a husband must provide for his wife in sickness and in health. And finally, he must accept his wife's work with gratitude, not demanding too much from her and giving her freedom to manage the affairs of the home.

The wife's duties. The Puritans taught that a wife, in addition to showing submission and reverence to her husband and fulfilling mutual marital duties, has numerous unique responsibilities. As a helpmeet for her husband, she should assist him in a variety of ways. These include helping him in his work, managing the affairs of the home, being thrifty without being miserly, and conducting herself with sobriety, mildness, courtesy, and modesty.

Conclusion: Marriage Based upon God's Word

The Bible was the Puritans' instruction manual for marriage—its purposes, principles, and practices. As J. I. Packer says, "They went to Genesis for its institution, to Ephesians for its full meaning, to Leviticus for its hygiene, to Proverbs for its

---

5. Gouge, *Of Domesticall Duties*, 225.
6. Herbert W. Richardson, *Nun, Witch, Playmate: The Americanization of Sex* (New York: Harper & Row, 1971), 69.

management, to several New Testament books for its ethic, and to Esther, Ruth, and the Song of Songs for illustrations and exhibitions of the ideal."[7]

No doubt many Puritan marriages fell considerably short of the ideal. Yet, the Puritans' view of an ideal marriage and their diligence, in dependence on God, to work toward that ideal made the foundations of their homes solid. They believed God's promise that the man who fears God and walks in His ways will be blessed with a happy marriage (Ps. 128:3).

---

7. J. I. Packer, *A Quest for Godliness: The Puritan Vision of the Christian Life* (Wheaton, Ill.: Crossway, 1990), 263.

40

Child-Rearing

The Puritans, both in writing and by example, provide us with the ideal Reformed Christian home. They believed, according to Scripture, that the family was the fundamental unit of human society. Well-ordered families, Cotton Mather says, "naturally produce a good order in other societies." He concludes, "Families are the nurseries for Church and Commonwealth; ruin families and you ruin all."[1] A high premium, therefore, was placed on raising children in a God-honoring way.

Child-Rearing from Conception

For the Puritans, child-rearing begins at conception. Prospective parents had two major tasks before a child was born. First, they were to pray daily for the salvation of their child, since the child was conceived in sin (Ps. 51:5). They also were to pray daily for the protection of both mother and child.

Second, since miscarriages were nearly as common then as they are today, the health of the mother was to be carefully protected. Husbands were expected to care for and help their wives during pregnancy and childbirth. Mothers, likewise, were to take great care in matters of physical health so as to prevent miscarriage.

Child-Rearing Covenantally

With rare exceptions, Puritan child-rearing was rooted in the conviction that children belonged to the covenant which God makes with believers and their seed (Acts 2:39; 1 Cor. 7:14), as confirmed in baptism, which, being a sacrament, is a visible sign and seal of God's invisible grace. The Puritans taught that just as the believing Israelite had to circumcise his son in the old covenant, so, in the new covenant, believing Christians are to present their children for baptism to

---

1. Quoted in Carden, *Puritan Christianity in America: Religion and Life in Seventeenth-Century Massachusetts* (Grand Rapids: Baker, 1990), 175.

confirm their inauguration into the covenant of grace. God, therefore, claims these children as His own; parents are stewards of their children on God's behalf. While this is so, the Puritans did not believe that their children were saved from birth or by baptism. They taught that their children were *in*, but not necessarily *of*, the covenant. They lived under the promises of the covenant, but they still needed to appropriate these promises through faith. Hence, parents were to evangelize their children, stressing with them the need to be born again, evidenced by repentance, faith in Christ, and a holy walk.

Child-Rearing for Salvation and Godliness

According to Isaac Ambrose, parents have the task of "erecting and establishing Christ's glorious kingdom in their house."[2] The Puritans stressed that children must be trained early in the nurture and admonition of the Lord.

Education. The Puritans made it a law that parents must teach their children to read so that they could read the Bible and other religious material for their spiritual welfare. They used a catechism (a series of questions and answers explaining fundamental Christian doctrines) to instruct their children as soon as possible. The goals of catechizing were to make sermons and the sacraments more understandable for covenant children, to prepare them for confession of faith, and to teach them how to live as Christians and defend their faith against error. The ultimate goal, however, was not simply a well-stocked head, but also a growing appetite for and appreciation of the truths of God in mind and soul so that the child would lead a holy life.

Family Worship. Puritan families gathered for worship once or twice each day. This was the most powerful means for child-rearing. Typically, Puritan family worship included four elements. First, there was prayer. They confessed family sins, asked for family mercies, and offered family thanksgivings. Second, there was reading of Scripture. The family usually read straight through the Bible, out of the conviction that God gave a whole Bible to make a whole Christian. Third, there was instruction from Scripture. The Puritans believed that the father should interact with his family about sacred truth on a daily basis by means of questions, answers, and teaching. Finally, there was praise, the singing of psalms "with grace in the heart."

---

2. Quoted in R. C. Richardson, *Puritanism in North-West England: A Regional Study of Chester to 1642* (Manchester: Manchester University Press, 1972), 105.

Child-Rearing by Discipline

The Puritans held that firm discipline was an essential part of child-rearing. Such discipline involved more than teaching and modeling proper behavior. Reproof plus the rod gives wisdom, the Puritans said. When a young child is disobedient, verbal reproof must be administered first. In this, the parent shows the child that he or she has committed sin against God and man and must repent. If verbal reproof is ineffective, the rod must be used as "a means appointed by God," Gouge says, "to help good nurture and education of children. It is the last remedy that a parent can use: a remedy which may do good when nothing else can."[3] This, however, must be done in a timely manner, with love, compassion, prayer, consistency, self-control—and always only to the degree of the moral offense that was committed. Corrective discipline must never be administered in anger. It must also be administered with teaching to encourage understanding, faith, and repentance.

Discipline, however, should not only be corrective, the Puritans said, but also preventive. Thus, parents are to give clear scriptural guidelines to their children to direct them in the paths of obedience, as well as clear exhortations as to what their punishment will be when they violate those guidelines. They need to heavily invest in their children's lives, fostering a climate of love, fellowship, and conversation in their home. Above all, they need to walk with integrity before their children, as mentors of obedience to God.

Conclusion: Child-Rearing for God

Beginning with the premise that the Bible is a reliable repository of truth, the Puritans had a basis from which to apply their Christian faith to child-rearing. In every area, the parental task was to lead children to God and to do His will. Puritan parents prayerfully awaited God's blessing on their endeavors. Blessing was measured primarily by their children's walking in communion with God, manifesting holiness in their lives, and exercising their gifts to the well-being of family, church, and society.

---

3. Gouge, *Of Domesticall Duties*, 552.

41

Work as a Calling

The Puritan view of secular work is theologically rich. Two of the most extensive treatments on this subject are *A Treatise of the Vocations and Callings of Men* by William Perkins and *The Religious Tradesman* by Richard Steele. While these works address the idea of calling from different angles, together they provide a general framework for the way Puritans thought about this concept and how they practiced it in their daily lives. For both Perkins and Steele, the idea of work as a calling elevated secular work by giving it intrinsic value. A man's calling not only afforded him an arena to glorify God with his life but also an avenue to serve the common good with his unique talents and abilities.

Calling and Creation

Like the Protestant Reformers before them, the Puritans anchored their theology of work in the doctrine of vocation or calling. For Perkins the concept of calling grounded a man's secular work in the power and Lordship of God. He writes, "A vocation (or calling) is a certain kind of life, ordained and imposed on man by God for the common good."[1] From this definition, Perkins wants to emphasize that a person's calling, whether it be secular work or a calling to Christian ministry, begins first and foremost with God.

Perkins likens God's role in determining one's calling to that of a military general. Just as a general "appoints to every man his place and standing" so God appoints every man to a calling. And just as a solider is to "live and die" at his post, so every man ought to stay in his calling until the general tells him it is time to leave.[2] Thus, the Christian should not view his job as something that he has fallen into by random chance or by human choice; rather, every vocation is ordained and determined by God.

1. Perkins, *A Treatise on the Vocations*, in *Works*, 10:43.
2. Perkins, *A Treatise on the Vocations*, in *Works*, 10:44.

WORK AS A CALLING • 135

Richard Steele draws upon the doctrine of creation to establish human work as a divine mandate placed upon all men. Steele begins his work with a celebration of the various ways God has equipped men and women for different types of work. Some are fit for the work of the mind, "being endowed with extensive knowledge," others are given "penetrating judgment," still others a "curious hand" and a "strong arm" to do manual labor. With all these unique gifts, "the wise governor of the universe has appointed to every one his proper place and work, and will rather reprove than reward those who are acting out of their own sphere."[3] Man's job is to find his proper sphere and seek to glorify God in his work.

Because God has called and created us to live and work in a particular calling, the Puritans believed that, once we have discovered this calling, we should stay in it unless God tells us otherwise. Instead of seeking to move from one vocation to another, or becoming envious of another man's calling, Perkins advises that a man dedicate himself to his particular station in life with all diligence for God's glory and the common good.

The Common Good

Both Perkins and Steele employ the body metaphor to describe how God has designed callings to benefit the whole of society. Perkins explains, "In man's body there are sundry parts and members, and each [of these body parts] has its several use and office, which it performs not for itself, but for the good of the whole body."[4] When understood in this light, human work takes on new significance. A man's work not only glorifies God, but also enables the society around him to flourish.

General and Particular Calling

At the heart of the Puritan understanding of work is the distinction between the general and particular calling. The general calling is that which all who have become Christians received when they put their faith in Christ. This calling is rooted in our election in Christ by which we are called out from the nonelect to live a holy and godly life of faith and good works. As Perkins explains, "The general calling is that whereby a man is called out of the world to be a child of God, a member of Christ, and an heir of the kingdom of heaven."[5] The particular

---

3. Richard Steele, *The Religious Tradesman* (Trenton, N.J.: Francis Wiggins, 1823), 11–12.
4. Perkins, *A Treatise on the Vocations*, in *Works*, 10:45.
5. Perkins, *A Treatise on the Vocations*, in *Works*, 10:49.

calling is the expression of the general calling through a particular trade or office. For the Puritan, maintaining the correct relationship between the two callings is vitally important for living faithfully as a Christian in the world.

Perkins says that the general calling to Christian faith contains several duties that all Christians are obligated to perform: calling on God's name in prayer, serving to the good of the church, providing financially for God's causes, and loving one another. Particular callings, however, distinguish us from each other, so that we can work for the good of all with our particular gifts. Through our particular callings we are called to love and serve each other diligently, content with the gifts and calling God has given us. Consequently, everyone must have such a calling so as to employ his or her unique gifts and abilities. Perkins says that people without callings are like "rotten legs and arms that drop from the body."[6]

Following a Calling

Because of the high view of calling in the Puritan worldview, identifying and following a calling is a weighty matter requiring much discernment. Discerning the right calling did not just have ramifications for the enjoyment of this life, but also for the enjoyment of the life to come.

The Puritans advised that when discerning a calling, two vital questions should be considered: is the work lawful, and is it suitable? To determine if a calling is lawful, Steele proposes the following test: "Those only are lawful in which we can reasonably ask for the blessing of God, and expect his favor and acceptance."[7]

Concerning the fitness of the calling to one's particular gifts and talents, Perkins says that when people choose a work for which they are unfit, it is like a body that gets out of joint. It is just as bad for society as if they were engaged in an unlawful calling.[8] What, then, makes a man fit for a particular calling? Perkins has two main criteria: gifting and desire. One must first ask, what do I want to do? What do I have in my heart to do? Then one must ask, what am I good at? Where a man's desires and gifts come together, there he will find his calling.

Given the level of wisdom needed to discern the right calling, the Puritans placed a great responsibility on parents to help their children in the discernment process. Parents should observe the gifts and desires of their children, taking

---

6. Perkins, *A Treatise on the Vocations*, in *Works*, 10:55.
7. Steele, *Religious Tradesman*, 25.
8. Perkins, *A Treatise on the Vocations*, in *Works*, 10:61.

note of the activities to which they are drawn and in which they excel. Children with a strong physical constitution should be brought up to engage in more laborious callings. Children with strong minds should be moved towards intellectual pursuits.

Diligence in Our Calling

Given this view of work, it is of utmost importance for all people to approach their work with all diligence, for, as Perkins said, "labor in a calling is as precious as gold or silver."[9] The more diligence a person applies to his calling, usually the more God will bless him in it. On the other hand, if a man fails to use what God has given to him, even what he has will be taken away (Matt. 25:29).

For Perkins, diligence is not only important as a stewardship of God's gifts but also as a responsibility to one's community. God's glory and our debt to society are deep motivators for diligence in our calling.

Both Steele and Perkins argue that idleness and sloth lead to many other vices when they are allowed to fester in a man's life. When a man is slothful, the devil has a field day. Sin will begin to creep into his life.

Conclusion: Dignity to All Work

One important result of the Puritan view of calling is its power to give dignity to the most menial aspects of work. While there is a particularly high level of dignity that comes with a calling to the ministry, all lawful employments have great value or worth when they are viewed as divine callings. As William Tyndale says, "There is difference betwixt washing of dishes, and preaching the word of God; but as touching to please God, not at all."[10] For the Puritans, the idea of work as a "calling" offered more than simply the possibility of serving God while you are at work. It offered the possibility of "serving God through or by means of that work." In other words, work was not something a man did when he was not serving God, it was the means by which a man pleased God in and throughout his whole life.[11]

---

9. Perkins, *A Treatise on the Vocations*, in *Works*, 10:48.

10. William Tyndale, "The Parable of the Wicked Mammon," in *Doctrinal Treatises and Introductions to Different Portions of the Holy Scriptures*, ed. Rev. Henry Walter (Cambridge: Cambridge University Press, 1848), 102.

11. Leland Ryken, "The Original Puritan Work Ethic," *Christian History* 89 (2006): 33.

PART SEVEN

The Puritans for Today

42

Learning from Puritan Faults

We can also always learn from the weaknesses and blind spots of every movement—religious or secular—in church history. That is true of the Puritans as well.

No introduction to the Puritans would be complete without mentioning what we can learn from the Puritans' faults. Selecting faults can be rather subjective, of course, and we don't pretend to offer you a complete list of them. The Puritans themselves would no doubt include many more, as they were often hard in judging themselves, as their spiritual journals attest. Though they set the bar high for Christian living for themselves, they too, like all of us, failed in numerous ways.

Exaggerated Preparatory Requirements and Legalistic Tendencies

First, a few of the Puritans, in their zeal for purity of religion and daily life, went overboard in that zeal. On the one hand, this could result in demanding too many deep experiences of humiliation before a sinner could be saved—such as Thomas Hooker's emphasis on a preparatory sign of grace being that a convicted sinner must be willing to go to hell for God's glory.

On the other hand, a few Puritans also fell into forms of legalism, by stifling the liberty of a Christian's conscience in certain areas, such as recreational activities. Happily, the Puritans that fell into these particular errors were a small minority, but nonetheless they have done damage to the Puritan cause both in their own day and in ours. Long after their descendants had cast off the faith of the Puritans, the legalism was perpetuated in the cult of Victorian "respectability," based on nothing more than fear of what one's neighbors might think.

Intolerance of Others' Viewpoints

Second, at times some Puritans could be intolerant of those who differed from them. Dissenting voices were at times either exiled or oppressed. Though on occasion such treatment was justified given the attitude of the offenders, on other occasions the Puritans could have been more tolerant toward those who differed from them. This too has damaged the Puritan reputation.

This Puritan intolerance led to seeing very few things as indifferent. The Puritans commonly had viewpoints on nearly everything, and habitually grounded those viewpoints in the Scriptures—sometimes stretching their exegesis into eisegesis to prove their point. On the other hand, it must also be noted that their objections against a variety of things such as wedding rings, kneeling when receiving the elements of the Lord's Supper, and priestly vestments, hark back to their justified opposition to Roman Catholicism with all its unbiblical superstitions. And it must be remembered that their opponents were demanding conformity to such usages as a condition of church membership, public ministry, and civil liberty. Seen from the perspective of more than three centuries' distance, some of their severe opposition to matters that we might regard as indifferent or worthy of only mild opposition, leads us to regard the Puritans as being too partisan at times.

Slaves and Witch Trials

Third, some dreadful practices such as condoning the owning of slaves and conducting witch trials still mar the Puritan past. Though we can be grateful that both of these grievous problems infected only a small minority of the Puritans, even having one Puritan believe in such things is a serious blight. No amount of justification, including the idea that the few Puritans who owned slaves usually treated them well and evangelized them faithfully, can excuse this abominable practice. We are deeply grieved, ashamed, and embarrassed that any of the Puritans would ever have condoned slavery no matter what the rest of society was doing around them. They should certainly have known better.

As for witch trials, they too cannot be excused in any way. The spiritual maturity of a few of the Puritans who condoned it makes this serious blind spot all the more puzzling in our day. Again, it must be pointed out here, for the sake of historical accuracy, that most Puritans did not condone such harsh methods utilized against the supposed "witches." Ministers like Samuel Willard publicly detested the witch trials. Even judges like Samuel Sewall, who was prominent in the trials to a surprising degree, later repented of their involvement. Happily, some Puritans called for an end to the "spectral evidence" used, which helped end the trials.[1]

The Puritans as a whole have paid a heavy price for the sins of a minority among them in these areas. In spite of the careful studies and correctives of modern historians—secular and religious—the word Puritan is still used pejoratively by many as a synonym for harshness and superstition.

Other Weaknesses

Other Puritan weaknesses could be mentioned as well, though for some of these their historical context must be taken into account. Some would point to their zealous keeping of the entire Sabbath, whereas others would say that is one of their strengths.

Some would point to their spiritualizing and moralizing of everyday issues—particularly from parents to children, whereas others would respond that this is precisely where we fall short in our unspiritual and immoral age.

Some point to their prolixity (such as Joseph Caryl preaching more than 300 sermons on the book of Job, and Anthony Burgess preaching 145 sermons on John 17), but it is worth noting that though this would be unsuitable for our day, the Puritan mind functioned differently in this regard than our minds do. We train preachers to expound the context in the chapter from which they are preaching, but the Puritans, for better or worse, viewed the entire Bible as the context! Actually, when one reads William Gurnall's lengthy tome, *The Christian Armour*, on half a chapter in Ephesians 6, it is astonishing how little repetition and prolixity is involved. It is our opinion that some Puritans were indeed guilty of prolixity, but others who wrote large tomes actually wrote great classics (like Gurnall's book) that are eminently worthy of being read through in their entirety. Some Puritan preachers had the gift to sustain such treatments of the text; others were not so gifted. Today's preachers can learn from that, and must take care to consider what their gifts are and how they can be used to best advantage.

Lessons for Us Today

From all of this the Puritans teach us three important truths. First, our own blind spots and sins as Christians can do much damage to others and to ourselves. For example, what will even the secular world think one century from

---

1. For an account and analysis of the witch trials, see Dean George Lampros, "Season of Anguish: The Formal Proceedings Conducted during the Salem Witchcraft Hysteria of 1692," *Westminster Theological Journal* 56 (1994): 303–27.

now of Christians who condoned the barbaric practice in our day of murdering millions of babies in the womb? How we need to cry out to God to show us our blind spots and sins and repent of them by confessing and forsaking them without delay. "Search me, O God, and know my heart: try me, and know my thoughts: and see if there be any wicked way in me, and lead me in the way everlasting" (Ps. 139:23–24).

Second, we need to learn from Puritan history how much damage can be done to a movement by a minority in the movement who participate in the faults and sins briefly outlined above. How many books, for example, have been written on the Salem witch trials! How much damage these trials have done to the Puritan cause despite the small number of Puritans involved in them! As Christians, we need to always remember that our own sins and blind spots have the potential to do much harm to the church of Jesus Christ.

Third, as Leland Ryken helpfully summarizes, we should learn from Puritans' weaknesses and faults by remembering to:

- Value leisure and recreation as good in themselves for purposes of rest, celebration, and human enrichment.

- Be on guard against multiplying the rules that we add to our foundational moral principles.

- Practice the art of conciseness, leave some things unstated, choose quality of words over their quantity, and respect the attention span of an audience.

- Beware of overkill through too much moralizing.

- Avoid thinking in terms of male superiority.

- Rise above party spirit by differentiating between the principle of a thing and its abuse.

- Respect the religious feelings of people whose viewpoint we reject.

- Remember that accuracy of expression is better than overstatement, that mildness of expression gains more respect than belligerence, and that a good thing when carried too far becomes ridiculous.[2]

Finally, while it is true that the Puritans lived rather strict lives—especially when judged in terms of today's standards, and despite their blind spots—they

---

2. Leland Ryken, *Worldly Saints: The Puritans as They Really Were* (Grand Rapids: Zondervan, 1986), 201. In this chapter we lean on Ryken's insights and assessments.

possessed a profound sense of God's mercy and forgiveness. What the Puritans disdained was worldly thinking, living as though time and eternity were insignificant to the human soul. However, the classic picture of the Puritan as the *pilgrim* or *traveler to Zion* is only a partial view. The Puritans blended otherworldly aspirations with this-worldly usefulness. Each one strove to be the best husband, or wife, or son, or daughter, or worker, in accord with God's Word and to His glory. In short, each one strove to be the best citizen of both worlds, despite the blind spots and sins that were committed by a minority of them in the areas mentioned above.

So, let's not let the Puritans' faults blind us from what we can learn from them—both from their weaknesses and their strengths. Let's be determined to follow them insofar as they followed Christ (1 Cor. 11:1)—and no further!

43

Lessons from the Puritans for Today

We have written this book as an overflow of gratitude. From childhood and youth we each have found ourselves enriched, challenged, encouraged, and made a little wiser by reading Puritan literature. And our simple desire is to share that blessing, that others might enjoy the benefits of such a treasure trove.

Here are just a few reasons why we believe the Puritans are so valuable still today.

They Are Scriptural

Reading the Puritans, it is hard not to be struck by their knowledge and use of Scripture. Their sermons and writings are studded with biblical allusions, phrases, illustrations, and proof texts. The Bible was their supreme authority, and was always referenced as the yardstick against which their teaching could be tested. Charles Spurgeon said on this:

> I would quote John Bunyan as an instance of what I mean. Read anything of his, and you will see that it is almost like reading the Bible itself.... Prick him anywhere; and you will find that his blood is Bibline, the very essence of the Bible flows from him. He cannot speak without quoting a text, for his soul is full of the Word of God.[1]

To say that the Puritans were *biblical* is not to say that they were lumpishly *biblicist*. They were not superficial proof texters; nor were they afraid of exploring the great doctrines of the faith—doctrines like the Trinity that cannot be developed from individual texts. They were doctrinally rich as they were biblically anchored, and so tended to be wise, balanced, and sensible.

---

1. C. H. Spurgeon, *C. H. Spurgeon's Autobiography, Compiled from His Diary, Letters, and Records, by His Wife and His Private Secretary*, 1878–1892, vol. 4 (Toronto: Fleming H. Revell, 1900), 268.

They Are Christ-Focused

They also kept their doctrinal focus where Scripture does: on Christ. Richard Sibbes once described the aim of pastoral ministry in words that could very well apply to the Puritan movement as a whole:

> The main end of our calling, the ministry is to lay open and unfold the unsearchable riches of Christ; to dig up the mine, thereby to draw the affections of those that belong to God to Christ.... It is the end of our calling to sue for a marriage between Christ and every soul. We are the friends of the bride, to bring the church to him; and the friends of the church, to bring Christ to them.[2]

William Perkins put it even more succinctly, concluding his influential book on preaching with these words: "Preach one Christ by Christ to the praise of Christ."[3]

The Puritans found Christ everywhere in the Bible. According to Thomas Adams, "Christ is the sum of the whole Bible, prophesied, typified, prefigured, exhibited, demonstrated, to be found in every leaf, almost in every line, the Scriptures being but as it were the swaddling bands of the child Jesus."[4] Likewise, Isaac Ambrose wrote, "Think of Christ as the very substance, marrow, soul, and scope of the whole Scriptures."[5] Hence it was as natural for the Puritans to turn to the Old Testament as well as to the New in preaching Christ and instructing His people.

The Puritans loved Christ and wrote much about His beauty. The puritan-minded Samuel Rutherford wrote: "Put the beauty of ten thousand thousand worlds of paradises, like the Garden of Eden in one; put all trees, all flowers, all smells, all colors, all tastes, all joys, all loveliness, all sweetness in one. O what a fair and excellent thing would that be? And yet it would be less to that fair and dearest well-beloved Christ than one drop of rain to the whole seas, rivers, lakes, and foundations of ten thousand earths."[6] Thomas Goodwin echoed this thought by asserting that heaven would be like hell to him if Christ were not there.

---

2. Sibbes, "Bowels Opened," in *Works*, 2:142.

3. Perkins, *The Art of Prophesying, or, A Treatise Concerning the Sacred and Only True Manner and Method of Preaching*, in *Works*, 10:356.

4. Thomas Adams, "Meditations upon Some Part of the Creed," in *The Works of Thomas Adams* (1862; repr., Eureka, Calif.: Tanski, 1998), 3:224.

5. Quoted in Packer, *A Quest for Godliness*, 103.

6. Samuel Rutherford, "Epistle 29. To the Lady Kilconquhair," in *Joshua Redivivus, Or, Three Hundred and Fifty-Two Religious Letters, by the late eminently pious Mr. Samuel Rutherford, Professor of Divinity at St. Andrews* (Glasgow: William Bell, 1796), 60.

This focus on Christ saved the Puritans from many theological eccentricities—and suffused their writings with worship. Would you know Christ better and love Him more fully? Immerse yourself in Puritan literature, asking the Spirit to sanctify it to you in a Christ-centered way.

They Are Devotional

Tragically, the word "devotional" today is often a mild slur, meaning frothy and lightweight, something more "inspirational" than intellectual. None of these qualities apply well to the Puritans. The Puritans tended to be highly learned men, well-trained in linguistics, and well-educated in biblical, systematic, and historical theology. They had a depth and seriousness to their study, and great erudition as a result. Theirs tended to be a theology that stretches the mind.

Yet also, theirs tended to be a theology that inflames the heart. In Puritan hands, deep and thoughtful theology was never allowed to become a game for the intelligentsia—it fueled worship and it built up the church. They universally abhorred the sort of dead orthodoxy where doctrines get treated as mere balls in a game of theological ping-pong. They wanted to instill more than mere intellectual assent to the doctrines of the gospel; they wanted to see heartfelt knowledge of the truth. Thus, wrote John Owen in introducing his great treatise *Christologia*, "The great end of the description given of the person of Christ, is that we may love him, and thereby be transformed into his image."[7]

In fact, there is something about the Puritans that fills their writings and yet somehow goes even beyond their content. Writers in their day would have called it a "tincture"—an atmosphere or tone. They exude both prayerfulness and an awestruck wonder at the glory and grace of God.

They Are Practical

The Puritans were a people who longed to see the reformation of human hearts, minds, and lives by the Word of God. As such, they consciously sought to be pastoral and practical. It almost certainly helped that so many of them were also great sufferers, enduring levels of persecution, pain, and bereavement almost unheard of in the comfortable West today. They simply could not play at Christianity. In every part of life, they longed, preached, pastored, wrote, lived, and died to see God glorified and to prepare their souls to meet Christ on the Judgment Day clothed in His righteousness.

---

7. Owen, *Christologia*, in *Works*, 1:27.

Conclusion: Read the Puritans Prayerfully

For these reasons—and many more—you will find life-giving riches in the Puritans. And therefore we advise you, dear reader, take and read them, despite the fact that they too had their flaws and blind spots like we all do.

But we must go beyond studying their theology, discussing their ideas, recalling their achievements, and berating their failures. The real questions for us are: Are we, like the Puritans, thirsting to glorify the triune God? Are we motivated by biblical truth and biblical fire as they were? Do we share the Puritan view of the vital necessity of conversion and of being clothed with Christ's righteousness?

It is not enough to just read the Puritans. A stirring of interest in the Puritans is not the same thing as a revival of Puritanism. We need the inward disposition of the Puritans—the authentic, biblical, intelligent piety they understood, taught, and lived—we need that piety in our hearts, lives, churches, and nations.

Despite their failures, will we practice the degree of obedience to God's Word for which they strove? Will we confess in truth with them that there is more evil in one drop of sin than there is in the worst affliction? Will we love Christ the way they loved Him, and serve the triune God as they served Him? Will we live with one eye on eternity as they did?

Read the Puritans—carefully, meditatively, and prayerfully, and then go out and follow them insofar as they followed Christ (1 Cor. 4:16). You won't be sorry. If you're not saved, it may well lead, by the Spirit's grace, to your salvation. If you're saved, it will lead to your spiritual growth, holiness, and maturity.

44

How Should We Begin Reading the Puritans?

George Whitefield wrote about the Puritans and their writings as follows:

The Puritans [were] burning and shining lights. When cast out by the black Bartholomew Act, and driven from their respective charges to preach in barns and fields, in the highways and hedges, they in a special manner wrote and preached as men having authority. Though dead, by their writings they yet speak: a peculiar unction attends them to this very hour; and for these thirty years past I have remarked, that the more true and vital religion hath revived either at home or abroad, the more the good old puritanical writings, or the authors of a like stamp who lived and died in communion with the Church of England, have been called for....

Their works still praise them in the gates; and without pretending to a spirit of prophecy, we may venture to affirm that they will live and flourish, when more modern performances of a contrary cast, notwithstanding their gaudy and tinseled trappings, will languish and die in the esteem of those whose understandings are opened to discern what comes nearest to the Scripture standard.[1]

If you are just starting to read the Puritans, try beginning with the series of "Puritan Treasures for Today" published by Reformation Heritage Books. These are short Puritan works of about a hundred pages each in which every sentence has been edited (without sacrificing content!) in contemporary English so that they read like they were written yesterday. Begin, for example, with John Flavel's *Triumphing Over Sinful Fear*, William Greenhill's *Stop Loving the World*, and Anthony Burgess's *Faith Seeking Assurance*. This easy-to-read series will show you immediately how moving and deep the spirituality of the Puritans is compared to most of the shallow Christian material readily available in most Christian bookstores today.

---

1. George Whitefield, preface to *The Works of That Eminent Servant of Christ Mr. John Bunyan*, 2 vols., 3rd ed. (London: W. Johnston, 1767), 1:iii–iv.

Once you are hooked by the rich content of Puritan writings, move into reading original, unedited Puritan titles. We recommend beginning with Thomas Watson's *Heaven Taken by Storm*, John Bunyan's *The Fear of God*, John Flavel's *Keeping the Heart*, Thomas Brooks's *Precious Remedies against Satan's Devices*, and Richard Sibbes's *Glorious Freedom*; then move on eventually to the works of John Owen, Thomas Goodwin, and Jonathan Edwards, which will challenge you a bit more.

For sources that introduce you to the Puritan lifestyle and theology, begin with Leland Ryken's *Worldly Saints: The Puritans as They Really Were* (Grand Rapids: Zondervan, 1990), Peter Lewis's *The Genius of Puritanism* (Morgan, Penn.: Soli Deo Gloria, 1997); Erroll Hulse's *Who Are the Puritans? And What Do They Teach?* (Darlington, England: Evangelical Press, 2000); and James I. Packer's *A Quest for Godliness: The Puritan Vision of the Christian Life* (Wheaton, Ill.: Crossway Books, 1990). Then move on to Joel R. Beeke and Randall J. Pederson's *Meet the Puritans: A Guide to Modern Reprints* (Grand Rapids: Reformation Heritage Books, 2006), which provides you with short summaries of the lives of nearly 150 Puritans and a short summary of the 700 Puritan titles reprinted in the fifty-year span from 1956 to 2005, together with its matching volume by Joel R. Beeke and Mark Jones, *A Puritan Theology: Doctrine for Life* (Grand Rapids: Reformation Books, 2014), which provides you with the teaching of the Puritans in fifty different subject areas, and then shows you how the Puritans applied their teaching to various areas of their practical lives.